ESTRENO CONTEMPORARY SPANISH PLAYS

General Editors

Iride Lamartina-Lens and Susan Berardini
Modern Languages Department
Pace University, New York, NY

Advisory Board

Sharon Carnicke
Professor of Theatre
University of Southern California

Sandra Harper
Editor, *Estreno*
Ohio Wesleyan University

Marion Peter Holt
Critic and Translator
New York City

Steven Hunt
Director and Theatre Professor
Iowa City

Felicia Hardison Londré
Curators' Professor of Theatre
University of Missouri, Kansas City
American Theatre Fellow

Grant McKernie
Professor of Theatre
University of Oregon

Gabor Barabas
Executive Producer
New Jersey Repertory Company
Long Branch, New Jersey

Phyllis Zatlin
Professor of Spanish
Rutgers, The State University

ESTRENO Collection of Contemporary Spanish Plays

General Editors: Iride Lamartina-Lens and Susan Berardini

SKIN IN FLAMES

GUILLEM CLUA

SKIN IN FLAMES

(*La pell en flames*)

Translated from the Catalan
by
DJ Sanders

ESTRENO Plays
New York, New York
2008

ESTRENO Contemporary Spanish Plays 31
General Editors: Iride Lamartina-Lens and Susan Berardini
Modern Languages Department--PNY
Pace University
41 Park Row
New York, NY 10038 USA

Library of Congress Cataloging in Publication Data
Clua, Guillem, 1973-
  Skin in Flames
  Bibliography:
  Contents: Skin in Flames.
Translation of: La pell en flames.
  I.Clua, Guillem, 1973-
    Translation, English.
I. Sanders, DJ. II. Title.
Library of Congress Control No.: 2007937737
ISBN: 978-1-888463-27-9

© 2008 Copyright by ESTRENO
Original play ©Guillem Clua: La pell en flames, 2004.
Translation © DJ Sanders, 2006.

All rights reserved.
No part of this publication may be reproduced or transmitted in any form or by any means, electronic or mechanical, including photocopy, recording, or any information storage or retrieval system now known or to be invented, without permission in writing from the publishers, except by a reviewer who wishes to quote brief passages in connection with a review written for inclusion in a magazine, newspaper, or broadcast.

Cover Photograph courtesy of Jill Ritter, 2005
Cover: Jeffrey Eads

CAUTION: Professionals and amateurs are hereby warned that *Skin in Flames*, being fully protected under the Copyright Laws of the United States of America, the British Empire, including the Dominion of Canada, and all other countries covered by the Pan-American Copyright Convention and the Universal Copyright Conventions, and of all countries with which the United States has reciprocal copyright relations, is subject to royalty. All rights, including professional, amateur, motion picture, recitation, public reading, radio and television broadcasting, and the rights of translation into foreign languages, are strictly reserved. Particular emphasis is laid on the question of readings, permission for which must be secured in writing. No part of this publication may be reproduced, stored in a retrieval system, or transmitted, in any form or by any means, without the prior permission in writing of ESTRENO Plays.

Inquiries regarding permissions should be addressed to the author through:

Sociedad General de Autores y Editores
    Delegación General de Cataluña
    Paseo de Colón, 6
    08002 Barcelona, Spain
    e-mail: rmuntaner@sgae.es

or through the translator's agent:

The Susan Gurman Agency, LLC
865 West End Avenue, Suite 15A
New York, NY 10025
Ph: (212) 749-4618 Fax: (212) 864-5055
Susan@gurmanagency.com
    or
www.GurmanAgency.com

ABOUT THE PLAYWRIGHT

Guillem Clua (b. 1973) holds a degree in journalism from the Universitat Autónoma de Barcelona and has written articles and reports for several Catalan publications, including *TeatreBCN* and the daily newspaper, *El Periódico de Catalunya*. In 1994 he moved to England to study theatre at the London Guildhall University and became fluent in English. When he returned to Barcelona, he participated in the playwriting workshops and discussions conducted by leading Catalan playwrights and other theatre practitioners at the influential alternative theatre the *Sala Beckett*. His debut as a playwright came in 2002 when his stage adaptation of Thomas Mann's *Death in Venice* was performed at the Sala Muntaner. Two years later he won the Ciutat d'Alcoa Prize (Valencia) for his first full-length play, *Invisibles (The Invisible)*, establishing him as one of the most promising of a younger generation of Catalan dramatists.

Invisibles deals compellingly with the parallel relationships of six characters, ranging from a homeless man to a doctor whose indiscretions threaten her career. This mosaic of contemporary society reflects the varied but often unexpectedly interrelated lives in a large city. The play's inventive and scenically-challenging structure moves the action seamlessly between an abandoned subway station to a private residence to an ATM facility and other settings. All of the actors remain onstage continuously and assume their roles as the action requires. Clua himself has noted that his innovative play focuses on "the frontier between psychological normalcy and madness."

Clua's second play, *La pell en flames (Skin in Flames)* also won the Ciutat d'Alcoa Prize in 2004 and had a controversial staging at Barcelona's Villaroel Theatre in 2005, under the direction of

Carme Portaceli. It was subsequently staged in the United States by St.Louis's HotCity Company (2005) and the InterAct Theatre in Philadelphia (2007). While the play was not written as a provocative political statement, its depiction of the return of a Western photographer to the third-world country where he had captured an image on film of an anonymous girl in flames triggered associations with a famous photograph that has become synonymous with the debacle of the Viet Nam war. Again, the playwright experimented with scenic spatiality by presenting two actions simultaneously even though they are slightly separated in time.

In 2006, Clua completed *El sabor de las cenizas (The Taste of Ashes)*, written in Spanish, in which he again deals with conflict imposed by cultural differences as well as misunderstandings perpetuated by violence. Set in Jerusalem, the play depicts a fateful encounter between three Americans and two young Palestinians. In a brief time, new relationships develop between them as the action moves from a tourist hotel to the sacred sites of the city, and later to a Palestinian ghetto. The play reaches a violent climax but Clua has written a compelling coda, set beside the Dead Sea, which offers a surprising note of redemption.

Clua's most recent work, a one-act play entitled *Andròmeda*, was published in 2006 in a collection of children's plays by ten Catalan playwrights. Although brief, *Andròmeda* offers a fully developed dramatic situation with appealing poetic overtones.

Marion Peter Holt
Emeritus Professor of Theatre
CUNY Graduate Center

A NOTE ON THE PLAY

A sense of aching distance and suffering is palpable in this drama about the long-term fallout and cyclical nature of violent conflict. Set in the aftermath of war where the insidious damage inflicted in the past haunts the present, *Skin in Flames* focuses on the lives of four persons whose individual perspective of the past and present offer four different responses. The two women and two men are connected by past events and play out their personal tragedies in Guillem Clua's powerful and provocative study of human nature. Audience members quickly gain an intimacy with the characters, yet the intimacy is not uncomfortable; rather, it produces a shared experience between characters and spectators.

  The mimetic set of a shabby hotel suite forms the space of overlapping action among the characters. While Hanna, a journalist, interviews Frederick Salomon, a photographer whose iconic war photo taken twenty years earlier made him famous, Ida and Dr. Brown play out another drama. Brown is cold, indifferent, and brutal to Ida, his sexual chattel, when he is in town. Ida, whose young daughter is critically ill, represents the victim of war-torn country while Dr. Brown represents the victimizer who pillages wherever and whenever he can. The author sharply criticizes the unrelenting greed driven by capitalist ventures, and the trivialization of catastrophe by mass media. Although the Western world is mentioned a number of times, the key to *Skin in Flames* turns on its absence of temporal, geographic, or linguistic restrictions.

  A child literally set afire by the blast of a bomb is the subject of the photo taken by Salomon. Both Ida and Hanna have severe burn scars on their neck and back, leading the spectator and/or reader to focus on which, if either, of the women could be the child from that frightening moment twenty years earlier. Clua does suggest that it is Ida rather than Hanna. Yet, solving the puzzle of the identity of the child misses the point. At a more profound level, *Skin in Flames* only makes sense when we see that Clua points out that many children are scarred both physically and emotionally from the burn of an enemy's hatred. Not only that, but many others are willing to benefit at the expense of the victims. Furthermore, the author stresses the cyclical nature of violence not merely by closing the drama with the opening lines and action, but also by setting the action at "midday". Morning suggests the dawning of peace and regeneration as the logical outcome of a war's conclusion, but what we see in this play at midday suggests that no lasting peace or renewal can ever come about. Rather, it seems that twilight will be the eve of further destruction, be it of the technological or political category. With a set that casts "a lasting image of filth", the future cannot be bright.

Through varying degrees, both Salomon and Dr. Brown have sold their souls for celebrity and fortune, yet Hanna and Ida warrant further analysis. Ida is submissive to Brown's sexual prurience in order to save her young daughter who, it turns out, died the previous night while comatose in the hospital. Brown has cruelly withheld this fact from the young and desperate mother until he satisfies his own carnal appetite. We see Ida nude on stage, performing explicit sex acts on Brown, but she is no vapid hussy. Completely debased and demoralized, Ida joins her daughter by lunging from the tenth-floor hotel suite window to her death. Hanna, a college-educated, professional woman, verbally accuses Salomon of moral perfidy as she interrogates him. But the author has saved the best for last. The effectiveness of the drama depends on the element of surprise. Hanna is convincing when she claims to be the child in the photo, showing her scars to an initially skeptical Salomon who asks for further proof. Pretending to believe her and knowing that the world has been awaiting the identification of the child in the photo, Salomon persuades Hanna to accompany him to the luncheon where he will receive an international award with a one-million dollar purse attached. She agrees, but as they prepare to depart, Salomon offers some corrections to her story, thus revealing that he knows she is not the girl in the photo, but an imposter eager to create her own celebrity and fortune.

There is no doubt that we feel sympathy for Salomon, particularly when he finds the photo of Ida's daughter as the action closes and recognizes her face from twenty years ago. Yet, the author is clear about the propensities of human nature. The questions that we consider are numerous. Do we indict Salomon or Hanna? Is the young woman just desperately seeking a means of survival within a system that rewards national loyalty and censures those who fail to conform? Is it the nature of the human condition that some individuals are casualties and others opportunists? Given the fact that the action is cyclical, should we or can we expect any conversion of humanity in order to replace venal self-interest with altruistic conscience? Ultimately, the "skin in flames" signifies our own complicity as century after century we destroy those around us, whether by violence, indifference, or self-righteous platitude.

Candyce Leonard
Wake Forest University

DIRECTOR'S NOTE

I read dozens of plays each year as I try to program future seasons for my theatre, InterAct, in Philadelphia. Most of what I read is by authors with whom I am well-acquainted, or plays that have been referred to me by a colleague in the field. *Skin in Flames* was one of those rare plays that appeared to us, as if from "out of the blue." I had never heard of Guillem Clua (or any other contemporary Spanish or Catalan writer, for that matter) nor of his English translator, DJ Sanders.

  Like most artistic directors, I have very particular taste: I am drawn to works that examine important and provocative issues, expose humanity in its most compelling moments, and challenge our often comfortable political, social and cultural assumptions. I had barely finished reading the last devastating page of *Skin in Flames* when I knew we had to produce this play, and that I would direct it. Here was a story that thoroughly disturbed and transported me, taking me on a journey full of gut-wrenching surprises and revelations.

  The political terrain of the play – the exploration of journalistic ethics, the brutality of American (or Western) involvement in the "third world," the mass marketing of war, the underside of emerging democracies – would be enough to make an engaging evening of theatre. But Guillem Clua offers so much more than the familiar issue-driven drama. He has fashioned a stylishly spare and cyclical story that is more reminiscent of *film noir* than any piece of live theatre I have ever read or seen on stage. Split scenes seem to be played out in two identical hotel rooms at the same time; or is it the same hotel room at different times? No less memorable are Clua's characters: Frederick

Salomon, the world renowned American photographer whose 20 year-old photograph haunts his every moment; Hannah, the driven yet psychologically damaged journalist who interviews him; Dr. Brown, the deceptively brutal American diplomat; and Ida, perhaps the most singularly tragic figure ever written for the stage.

The most formidable challenge in directing *Skin in Flames* was creating the mysterious, driving, haunting "feel" of the play, as it pulls the audience slowly and deliberately toward its shocking conclusion. The great joy of directing *Skin in Flames* was that the play's surprises continued to deliver a dramatic punch even when I knew what was coming. But there can be nothing like that first encounter of the play – as a reader, or as an audience member (I can only assume) – which leaves one, literally, breathless.

Seth Rozin
Director
InterAct Theatre

Guillem Clúa. Photo courtesy of InterAct Theatre Co.

Cast of the InterAct Theatre production in Philadelphia, 2007, directed by Seth Rozin. Leah Walton as Hanna, Buck Schirner as Frederick Salomon, Charlotte Northeast as Ida, and Joe Guzmán as Dr. Brown. Photo courtesy of InterAct Theatre Co.

Charlotte Northeast as Ida, and Joe Guzmán as Dr. Brown in the 2007 InterAct Theatre production. Photo courtesy of InterAct Theatre Co.

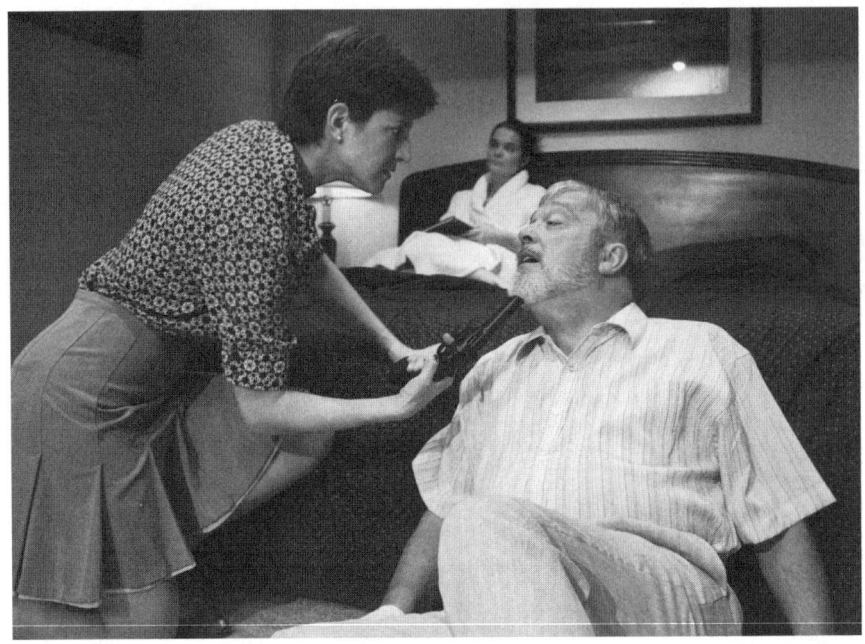

Leah Walton as Hanna, Buck Schirner as Frederick Salomon, and Charlotte Northeast as Ida in the 2007 InterAct Theatre production. Photo courtesy of InterAct Theatre Co.

Leah Walton as Hanna and Buck Schirner as Frederick Salomon in the 2007 InterAct Theatre production. Photo courtesy of InterAct Theatre Co.

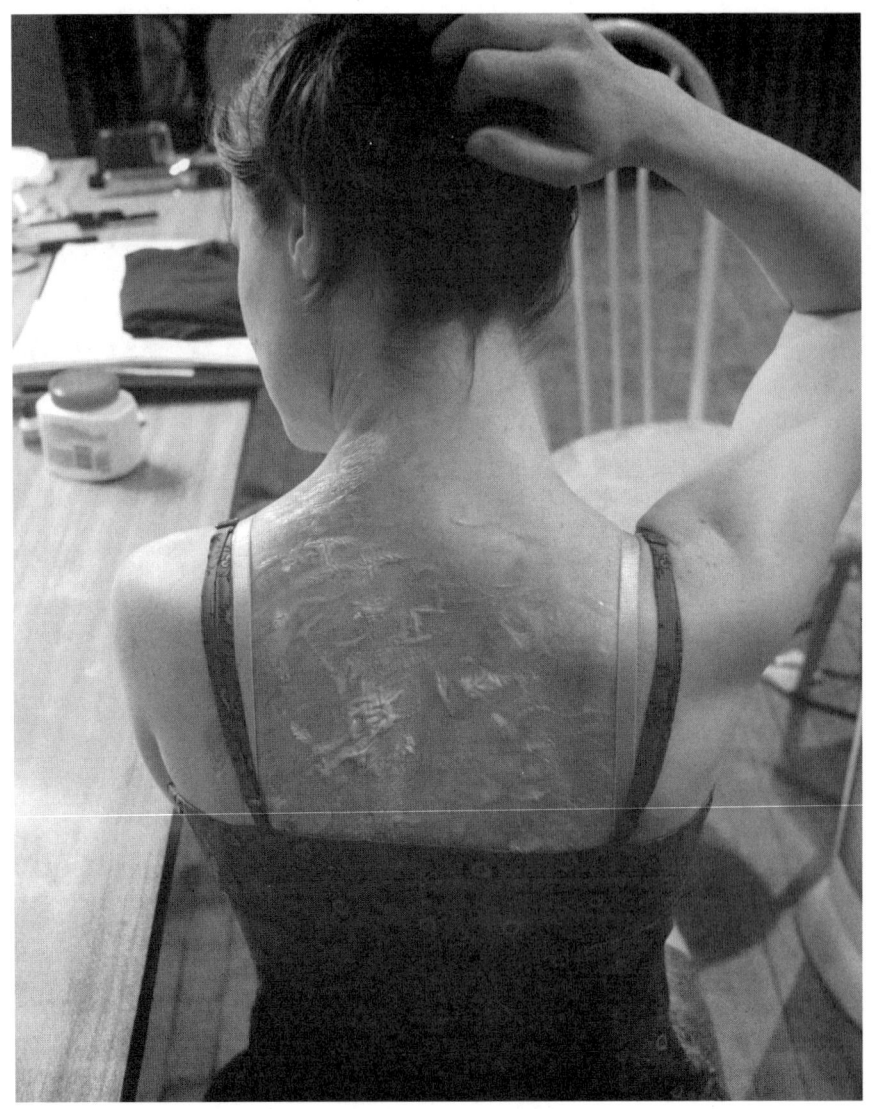

Julie Layton as Ida in the Hot City Theatre production in St. Louis, 2006, directed by Jason Cannon. Photo courtesy of Jill Ritter.

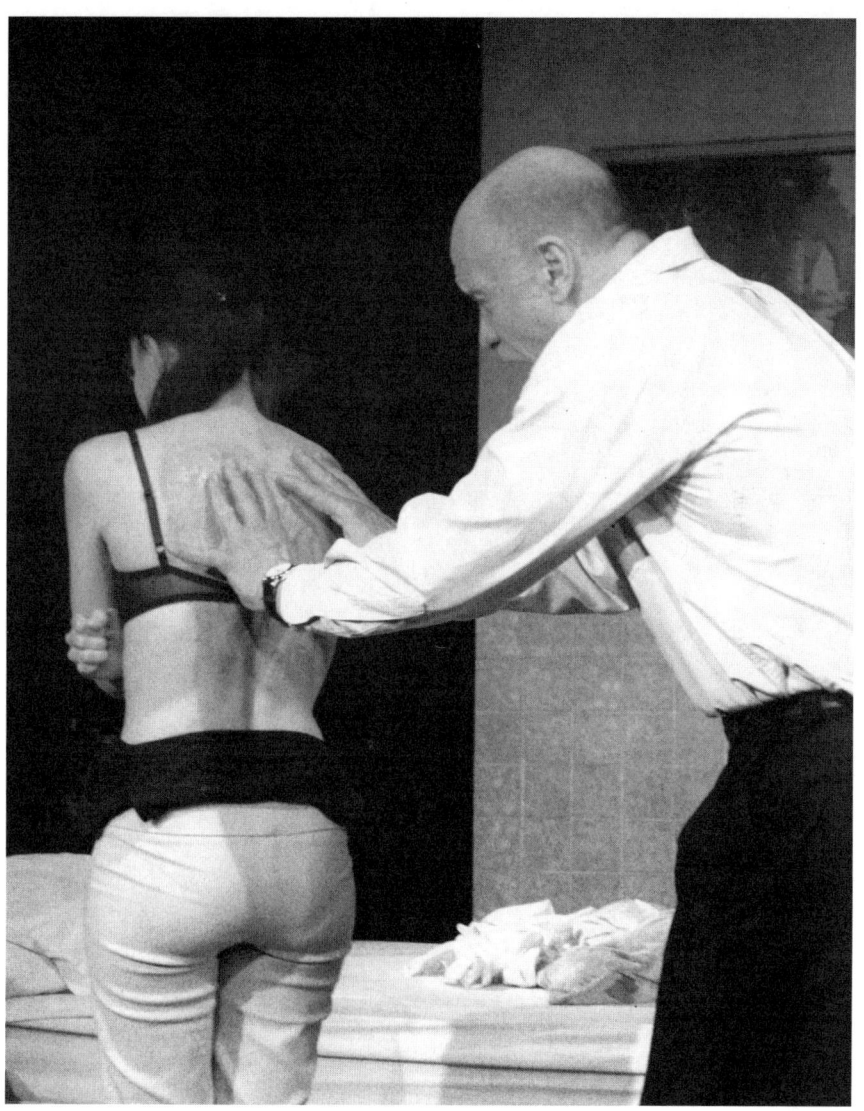

Sarah Cannon as Hanna and Peter Mayer as Frederick Salomon in the 2006 Hot City Theatre production. Photo courtesy of Jill Ritter.

Julie Layton as Ida in the 2006 Hot City Theatre production. Photo courtesy of Jill Ritter.

La pell en flames (*Skin in Flames*), directed by Carme Portaceli, premiered at the Villarroel Theatre in Barcelona, Spain on June 29, 2005. It won the 2004 Alcoi Theatre Prize as well as the 2005 Serra d'Or Critics Award for Best Script. In March, 2006, under the direction of Jason Cannon, *Skin in Flames* made its US debut at Theatre at St. John's in St. Louis, Missouri. The show was produced by HotCity Theatre in their Greenhouse Series. 2007 marked the east coast premiere of *Skin in Flames,* directed by Seth Rozin, at the InterAct Theatre in Philadelphia. Dramatic readings of *Skin in Flames* have been done at the Martin E. Segal Theatre Center in Manhattan (2006), and at the NJ Repertory Theatre in Long Branch, New Jersey (2008).

CHARACTERS:

FREDERICK SALOMON
HANNA
DOCTOR BROWN
IDA

TIME: Now.

SETTING:
A hotel suite in a post-war country. The room is notably western in décor, although dated and lacking charm. Upon first glance, the complete state of disarray leaves a lasting image of filth.

In the foreground, there is a small sitting room with standard furnishings including a small refrigerator with minibar service. A door leads to the exit. An archway with hung curtains separates the sitting room from the bedroom. In the bedroom there is a full-size bed and a large window with a small table in front of it.

RUNNING TIME:

The play runs approximately 80 minutes with no intermission.

AUTHOR'S NOTES

The hotel suite is the setting for two simultaneous scenes: one between Salomon and Hanna, the other between Brown and Ida. Both pairs occupy the same space without knowledge of the other.

Ida speaks with an accent and not as fluently as the other three characters. An accent should be created for her without making her recognizably from any particular country. Similarly, the country where the action takes place should remain ambiguous.

The character of Dr. Brown is tender and considerate with Ida at all times. He should come across as both friendly and paternal unless the stage directions indicate the contrary. Despite everything, he must be captivating.

The action is to be played naturalistic with the characters speaking to each other, not to the audience

Midday. The window is wide open. A gust of wind blows the curtains. Bright sunlight shines in on the unmade bed. Periodically, the sound of a car is heard from the sparse city traffic.

Suddenly, a woman screams from outside at the street level ten floors below. A cloud softens the invading sunlight. Silence. The door opens. FREDERICK SALOMON, a man of about fifty, enters with a suitcase. He wears a beige linen suit and white gloves. He moves about with confidence and purpose despite his being overweight and walking with a limp. Behind him enters HANNA, a woman in her late twenties, petite, and petulant, but with an inexplicable allure. She has done her best to dress elegantly with a blouse and skirt, but the cheap knockoff outfit fails to impress. She remains a suspicious woman watching her every step as if she feared the floor would fall out from under her feet. She carries a large handbag.

SALOMON: (*Indignant*): The best hotel in town. Isn't that what they said? The best hotel in town and they make you carry your own luggage to your room. (*To HANNA.*) Come in, come in. Don't stay out there. They'll think that... Just, come in.

(*HANNA enters and closes the door, but does not sit. SALOMON notices the disheveled sheets with a white bathrobe on top of them. He leaves his suitcase on the floor and sets a stack of papers on the table.*)

SALOMON:: And on top of that. Who the hell is running this place? (*To HANNA.*) Did you hear what they said about this room? You were right there with me. The best suite of the best hotel in town. Now I've seen it all.

HANNA: Things are different here than in your country, Mr. Salomon.

SALOMON: Unfortunately, things here are different than in any other country in the world.

(*SALOMON looks about the room with disgust. He turns*

toward the window suddenly as if something were calling his attention. For a moment, he is taken with fear.)

HANNA: Are you all right, Mr. Salomon?

SALOMON: No . . . For a moment it seemed like . . .(*SALOMON takes a deep breath and shakes his head to calm his anxiety. He grabs the bathrobe taking it into the bathroom where he lets out a groan of displeasure. He returns holding some blue panties at arm's length. He goes to the telephone. (To HANNA.)* Please, make yourself comfortable, if that's possible. (*HANNA does not sit and stays close to her bag. SALOMON picks up the phone and dials. On the phone.)* Yes. Frederick Salomon . . . Yes, I'm good, thank you . . . No. Absolutely not. This room's a pig sty... Why should that concern me? It looks like someone just left this room two seconds ago . . . Five minutes? Five western minutes or five local minutes?. . . Well, I hope so. Thank you. Goodbye. (*SALOMON hangs up. He shakes his head in disapproval of the panties, tossing them in the trash. To HANNA.)* Sorry, I didn't think that . . . If you like, we could do the interview somewhere else, perhaps somewhere more sanitary.

HANNA: No, it's fine.

SALOMON: Are you certain?

HANNA: Right here is fine.

(*SALOMON removes his jacket. SALOMON is visibly warm. He meticulously folds his jacket before setting it down in a place that he dusts off.*)

SALOMON: I really don't have that much time. In about a half hour they're coming to get me for the ceremony and lunch at the presidential palace with . . . well, I'm sure you already know . . . with all the members on the committee, a few dozen ambassadors, and the Minister of "I don't know what".

HANNA: The Minister of Tourism and Communication.

SALOMON: That's it. I see that you've done your homework.

HANNA: That is my job.

SALOMON (*Motioning to the suitcase.*): Do you mind if I...?

HANNA: Please, go ahead.

SALOMON: Can I offer you anything while you wait?

HANNA: No, I'm fine, thank you. (*SALOMON grabs his suitcase and opens it on the bed. He unpacks his clothes, putting them in the closet.*) You know I've been dreaming of doing this interview for years.

SALOMON: Thank you.

HANNA: It really means a lot to me.

SALOMON: Now which paper did you say you worked for?

HANNA: Which one do you think? We only have one national newspaper.

SALOMON: What happened to the other one?

HANNA: They closed it down last month for being unpatriotic.

SALOMON: Really? I'm so sorry to hear that.

HANNA: Why?
SALOMON: I don't know . . . Aren't *you* sorry?
HANNA: It wasn't *my* newspaper they shut down.
SALOMON: Even still . . .
HANNA: When *was* the last time you were here?
SALOMON: Twenty years ago.
HANNA: And after all this time have you noticed many changes?
SALOMON: A democracy has been instated.
HANNA: A democracy that also shuts down newspapers.
SALOMON: But in the end, it is a democracy. Your people should be proud. Especially you.
HANNA: Me?
SALOMON: How old are you? Twenty-five? Thirty? You've lived the majority of your life in wartime. Now, however . . .
HANNA: We're still living in wartime, Mr. Salomon. Just because you don't hear the bombs exploding doesn't mean the war is over.
SALOMON: But now you have the peace treaty.
HANNA: If you can call it that.
SALOMON: What else would you call it?
   (*HANNA gives no response. Pause. SALOMON has finished putting his clothing and suitcase in the closet.*)
HANNA: Are you expecting me to thank you?
SALOMON: For what?
HANNA: For the peace.
SALOMON: Thank *me*?
HANNA: Yes, you, your country, the United Nations. What's the

difference?
SALOMON: Don't be ridiculous.
HANNA: That's why they're giving you the award, isn't it?
SALOMON (B*itterly*): I didn't do anything.
HANNA: Yes, I know that.

(*Pause. SALOMON and HANNA size each other up with sudden suspicion. A strong breeze blows the curtains and causes some of the papers to fly off the table.*)

SALOMON: Shit. (*SALOMON rushes to collect the papers. He returns them to their original spot on the table and goes to close the window. He hesitates and first looks out the window to survey below. Quickly taken aback, a terrified SALOMON looks at HANNA before returning to look below.*) There's a woman down on the street. She's . . .

(*HANNA approaches the window and looks out and below.*)

HANNA (*Expressionless*): She's naked.
SALOMON: She's dead.
HANNA: She must have jumped from one of the hotel windows.
SALOMON: But . . . how long do you think that . . .
HANNA: It's the tallest building in the city. Some people come here just to ensure an easy death.

(***SALOMON*** *goes over, grabs the phone, and dials.*)

SALOMON (*On the telephone*): Yes, Frederick Salomon . . . Forget the damn room! There's a dead woman below on the lawn! Has anyone even noticed? . . . I don't know. Why don't you try calling an ambulance! . . . Yes, on the west side of the building . . . Well, I hope so. (*Hanging up, SALOMON returns to the window. HANNA has moved off to the side but remains focused on him. He remains fixed on the action below.*) Let's see if they get their asses in gear . . . How is it possible that . . . For the love of God! (*Pause. SALOMON's attention remains on the action outside below. Meanwhile, HANNA places herself behind him.*) Now they're finally out there.

(*HANNA pulls a handgun from her bag and points it at SALOMON.*)

SALOMON: A young woman... I'd say she's around your age, but I can't be sure. Poor girl. (*Pause. SALOMON continues looking outside. HANNA cocks the gun without SALOMON noticing.*) They're taking her inside. Do they call an ambulance? Of course not. Publicity like that wouldn't be good for the city's best hotel.

HANNA: This is fairly common. People die. No one asks questions.

(*At this moment, IDA enters the room from the bathroom. IDA appears to be the same age as HANNA and is dressed in a conservative yet appealing blue dress. IDA wears her long hair loose, allowing it to hide her neck and back. IDA stops between HANNA and SALOMON to toss and fix her hair. IDA is unaware of the others' presence as are they to her presence. HANNA continues to point the gun as it shakes in her hands. With his back still turned, SALOMON remains unaware.)*

SALOMON: I was so close to not even coming here, you know? Because of this. Death. And this day in particular. But you should know about that. You've done your research. That's your job. And for all this: the award. It's one thing to see it all on TV, but to see it here . . . *SALOMON cuts himself off, as if about to cry, but he holds it back. Pause. HANNA lowers her weapon, returning it to her handbag. IDA checks the time and looks out the window, next to SALOMON, as if waiting for someone.)* It's like nothing happened. A woman just killed herself and people go on like it's any other day. . .

HANNA: People are still afraid of getting too close to the windows.

(IDA sticks her head out the window and looks around.)

SALOMON: I shouldn't have . . . Look, someone else is looking out their window a few floors down. She's wearing a beautiful dress.

(*A knock at the door. IDA goes to open the door and fixes her hair along the way. SALOMON pulls back to close the window, truly affected by what he has seen.*)

SALOMON: If you'll excuse me a moment . . . We can start the interview in a bit. Go ahead and make yourself comfortable. I'll . . . (*SALOMON cuts himself off and goes into the bathroom, closing himself inside. IDA opens the hotel room door. DOCTOR BROWN, a man in his forties who fears getting older, enters the room. His clothing, mannerisms, and the kiss he plants on her cheek come across as paternal and chivalrous. He carries a briefcase.*)

BROWN: Hello, sweetheart.
IDA: Hello, Dr. Brown.
BROWN: Did they let you in without any trouble?
IDA (*Worried*): Like always. I want to ask you how . . . ?
BROWN: How am I? I'm good, very good.
IDA: Sara.
BROWN: Ah, yes. She's still in intensive care.
IDA: But she is better?
BROWN: No change.
IDA: When can I see her?
BROWN: It's still early, Ida.
IDA: But . . .
BROWN: We need to keep her isolated.
IDA: I don't understand why they do this to me.
BROWN: It's better for her.

IDA: It's better for her that she be with her mother.

(*HANNA approaches the bathroom to listen outside the door.*)

BROWN: Are you complaining?
IDA (*Submissive*): No.
BROWN: Yes, you are complaining and there is no reason.
IDA: No. I am not complaining. I am very thankful.
BROWN: That's better.
IDA: But I . . .I only want to give her a little kiss. To be by her side.
BROWN: Remember that any infection could be fatal. Is that what you want? To kill her with one of your kisses? (*No response from IDA. BROWN sees that his comment has not been well received. HANNA goes to SALOMON's jacket, fishes out his wallet, and looks through it.*) We're doing everything we can.
IDA: I'm sorry.
BROWN: It's all right. (*IDA goes over to the bed where she lovingly pulls out a storybook that has been tucked in under the sheets.*)
IDA: I brought you her favorite storybook. Maybe you can give it to a nurse there or . . . I don't know. She likes you to read it before she go to sleep.

(*HANNA pulls a large sum of money out of the wallet and counts it. After returning the money to the wallet, she pulls out a photograph that grabs her attention.*)

BROWN: Ida . . .

IDA: The main character is a little pig. A little pig that travels in a balloon to find other animals. Sara likes it when you imitate the animals. Will you tell the nurse to imitate them? If she does not imitate them, the story is not funny.

BROWN: I can't promise anything.

IDA: She will hear it, right? She can hear it even if she is
Still . . .like that. I read it one time in a magazine.

BROWN: Of course she can.

(*The sound of the bathroom door opening can be heard. HANNA quickly puts back the photo and wallet. SALOMON emerges from the bathroom where he has washed his face and taken no notice of her snooping.*)

SALOMON: We can start whenever you like.

IDA: We can start whenever you like.

HANNA: If you're not feeling well . . .

BROWN: If you're not feeling well . . .

SALOMON (*Shaking his head no*): It's just the weather. This damn heat. It's going to my head. (*IDA shakes her head no and goes over to the bed. Once there, she slowly and submissively begins to undo the top of her dress to reveal a blue bra.*

BROWN *sets his briefcase down to watch her sitting.*) It'll probably be best if we got this over with as soon as possible. Do you have your tape recorder?
HANNA (*Sitting and pulling out a notepad and pen*): I'll just take notes.
SALOMON: If so, I trust that you'll let me read the interview before you publish it.
HANNA: If you like.

(*BROWN approaches IDA and caresses her skin softly. He begins to kiss her, at first delicately, then with increased passion.*)

SALOMON: I'm ready whenever you are.
HANNA: Why are you wearing gloves?
SALOMON: Excuse me?
HANNA: Especially with this heat. I'm surprised.
SALOMON: This is part of the interview?
HANNA: Yes.
SALOMON: I have...eczema. It's not. . . . it's not pretty.
HANNA: How long have you had it?
SALOMON: Do we really need to talk about my hands?
HANNA: Those hands are important.

(*BROWN slides IDA's hand down to massage his crotch.*)

SALOMON: I don't see why.

HANNA: Your hands created the most famous photograph in history. I'd say that makes them important.

SALOMON: Then let's talk about the photograph. My hands are of no concern.

HANNA: Does the topic bother you?

SALOMON: Let me be clear on this: I don't want to answer any personal questions. If that's what you wanted, you should have let me know ahead of time. (*Pause. HANNA takes a deep breath, conceding to SALOMON. They resume their roles of journalist and interviewee.*)

HANNA: What do you think of our government deciding to present you with the first International Merit Award for Art?

SALOMON: Well, receiving it has given us a lot of pride, to me, my profession, and my country. The establishment of such an award is, without a doubt, a small part of the grand efforts your government is making to restore a normal democracy. (*Pausing to regroup, then continuing as if it were a canned response.*) Really, it's just a photograph, but I am aware of what it represents for your nation's recent past.

HANNA: What are you planning to do with the million dollar prize money?

SALOMON: I'm going to donate it all to support sanitation relief and reconstruction efforts.(*HANNA has not been taking any notes, which SALOMON notices.*) Didn't you say you were going to take notes?

HANNA: I'll take notes when you tell me something I don't already know. (*IDA and BROWN continue undressing each other like passionate lovers until they are down to their undergarments. As HANNA continues, she will periodically take down a few notes.*) Don't you find it all a little much?

SALOMON: What?

HANNA: A million dollars for a photo you took twenty years ago.

SALOMON: It's not just any photo. You said so yourself.

HANNA: Exactly. But they've already given you every possible award. Do you really think that you need any more publicity?

SALOMON: This award is not publicity. Not for me or the photograph.

HANNA: Of course not, but for this country, it is.

SALOMON: What do you mean?

HANNA: In this country, the infant mortality rate is fifty percent, more than a third of the population has already been infected with the AIDS virus, the schools are destroyed, the only thing that does work are the weapons factories . . . and our government creates an International Merit Award for Art, which they give to you, specifically to you. Doesn't that sound like one big marketing campaign?

SALOMON: Don't expect any compromising statements from me here.

HANNA: No one's asking that. I'm only interested in honest statements.

SALOMON: What do you want? For them to close down your paper too?

HANNA: The girl.
SALOMON: What girl?
HANNA: The girl in the photo. What side was she from?
SALOMON: That doesn't matter.
HANNA: She was from the losing side, the side that, now twenty years later, is in control.
SALOMON: I don't think you've ever really taken a good look at the photograph.
HANNA: I can assure you I have. More than I care to admit.
SALOMON: Then maybe you just didn't understand it.
HANNA: What is there to understand exactly?
SALOMON: Well, that the photograph knows no sides. It only shows what happened: a girl, six or seven years old, flying through the air because a bomb exploded right behind her.
HANNA: Only that?
SALOMON: It really doesn't matter who dropped the bomb or who the girl was. You have to see the essence of the image: an innocent victim of terror. That's why it's become a symbol.
HANNA: A symbol of what?
SALOMON: You should already know. A symbol of peace.
HANNA: That's what people outside this country think, yes. That a little girl with her hair and back in flames on the brink of death is a symbol of peace...

(*At this moment, BROWN and IDA are naked. This reveals for the first time a horrible burn scar on IDA's back. BROWN lies back on the bed. IDA kneels and begins to perform oral sex on him.*)

SALOMON: So for you it's not?
HANNA: No.
SALOMON: What *does* it symbolize for you?
HANNA: Revenge.
SALOMON: Revenge?
HANNA (*Nodding yes*): Our people's misfortune was converted into a frivolous symbol of Western guilt. And do I need to remind you *who* sold the bomb from your photo to the rebel guerillas?

(*Pause.*)

SALOMON: Why are you telling me all of this?
HANNA: Because it's the truth.
SALOMON: You know that I'm moments away from having lunch with the Minister of Tourism and Communication. I'm sure he wouldn't be very pleased to know that someone working at the regime's official newspaper thought this way.
HANNA: My national loyalty is without a doubt. And it will stand just as strong when they publish this interview.
SALOMON: Well you better get on it, otherwise you're not going

to have anything to publish. (*Checking his watch.*) You've only got another twenty minutes.

(*Pause. HANNA gives the impression of reviewing her notes.*)

HANNA: In all this time I've seen the photograph of the little girl everywhere. Everyone's cut it out of magazines and the paper, it's been on television . . . I know that in your country they've made millions of replicas putting them on t-shirts, hats, posters, everything. In fact, in some cities you'll even find it painted on murals along the streets. Am I wrong?

SALOMON: No.

HANNA: They've written books on it. You yourself have signed numerous copies. It's been the topic of doctoral dissertations and television programs . . . Some anti-globalization groups have put it on their flag. It's unprecedented.

SALOMON: Look, the same thing happened with the image of Che Guevara, more or less.

HANNA: That was not the same. Don't try being modest.

SALOMON: Fine . . . You're right, why deny it.

HANNA: Has this kind of reception made you happy?

SALOMON (*Nodding yes*): It's the highest honor a photographer could ever hope for. . . people making the image their own . . .

HANNA: . . . and mass market it.

SALOMON: What doesn't get mass marketed in today's world? Even peace gets mass marketed.

HANNA: There. You've just given me my headline.
SALOMON (*Taken aback*): You wouldn't dare.
HANNA: I'm only joking. (*SALOMON does not laugh.*) So that's the highest honor a photographer could hope for... And it was twenty years ago that you achieved that... And what have you done since?
SALOMON: I've continued working in my profession.
HANNA: But you couldn't go any higher now.
SALOMON: That wasn't necessary.
HANNA: And you never went back to being a war correspondent?
SALOMON: No.
HANNA: Why not?
SALOMON: Because of my leg.
HANNA: No other reason?
SALOMON: Look, Miss . . .
HANNA: There had to be other reasons, right?
SALOMON (*Sternly*): I have no intention of answering that question.
HANNA: If you don't answer my questions, I might have to invent your answers myself.

(*Pause. SALOMON wipes the sweat from his forehead with a handkerchief. He smiles and stands up, attempting to diffuse the tension.*)

SALOMON: You're good. I have to give you that. You really know how to put somebody on the spot.

HANNA: Thank you.
SALOMON: What are you still doing here, anyway?
HANNA: Excuse me?
SALOMON: You're a good journalist, young, you speak my language fluently, you don't support this regime . . . What the hell are you doing in this country?
HANNA: I was born here. And my people are buried here.
SALOMON: But don't you want a better life?
HANNA: What is a better life? More money?
SALOMON: For starters.
HANNA: If I wanted more money I'd take up performing oral sex on U.N. delegates.

(BROWN lets out a moan of pleasure.)

SALOMON: I don't believe you'd do that. (*HANNA does not respond, permitting only a half-smile.*) Either way, I'm not talking about money. I'm talking about living a more . . . dignified life with hot water and no restrictions on electricity. Wouldn't you like to have all of that? I mean...wouldn't you like to be . . . happier?
HANNA: Does it really interest you that much, or are you just trying to be amiable?
SALOMON: I am genuinely interested.
HANNA: Do you really think that no one can be happy here?
SALOMON: What do you think? (*Pause. HANNA begins writing something in her notebook.*) What are you

writing?

HANNA (*Reading*): Question: do you think that our people are happy? Response: recovering from a long and cruel war is difficult, but I am certain that the new government is doing everything in its power to guarantee the well-being of all members of society, regardless which side their loyalties lie.

SALOMON: I couldn't have said it better myself. But you still haven't answered my question.

HANNA: I think that's a little too personal to ask.

SALOMON: Like the questions you're trying to ask me now.

HANNA: I'm not the famous one here. (*SALOMON smiles. HANNA's intelligence impresses him, but he continues to keep her at arm's length.*)

SALOMON: What else do you want to know?

HANNA: Tell me about the photo. Tell me about the exact moment when you took it. What happened?

SALOMON: You can read that in any of the numerous books published on the topic.

HANNA: I'd rather hear you explain it yourself.

(*As they speak, SALOMON goes to the closet and pulls out a plastic cup from his suitcase, goes to the minibar, and pours himself a whisky in the plastic cup, despite there being a set of crystal glasses available.*)

(*BROWN lets out another moan of pleasure.*)

SALOMON: It was during the last days of resistance in the capital. The rebels controlled half of the country and had surrounded the city a few weeks earlier. Their taking over the city was only a matter of time. The air attacks were frequent. Each day there were two, maybe three of them.

(BROWN shifts in the bed, taken over with pleasure. BROWN continues to become more and more vocally excited as if it was SALOMON's story that was making his blood surge.)

SALOMON: That day I was at a school downtown. It was run by some missionaries. My job was to capture the daily routine of the children, of the teachers . . . of how they tried to keep on going with some semblance of normalcy. Basically, the human side of the war like you read in the Sunday paper magazine. Then all of a sudden, the sirens started sounding. Everyone ran to the bomb shelter. It wasn't far. I got distracted taking photographs and when I finally took notice of my surroundings, the planes were already overhead. I pushed on to the bomb shelter, but at the entrance, I stopped and looked back at the school. That's when I saw her. A little girl had been left behind. She ran out with a book under her arm. When she got to the middle of the plaza, she stopped. She had no idea which direction to go. All the buildings in ruins must have looked the same, the poor girl. She just stood still, lost . . . I grabbed my camera, focused, and just at that moment, a bomb fell on the school. The explosion was brutal. Everything was engulfed in flames and the force from the blast hurled the body of the little girl some thirty feet forward.

(BROWN achieves an orgasm.)

SALOMON: For a moment, for a just a millisecond, as she flew through the air . . . the little girl looked at me. She was looking at the camera. I didn't realize that until I developed the negative . . . I wanted to go to her, to help her, but there was an explosion right by me and I lost consciousness. That's why my leg is. . . *(SALOMON downs the whisky.)*

(IDA spits and wipes her mouth with the sheets.)

SALOMON: Only later did I find out that the resistance had been storing weapons in the schools and hospitals. That's why the explosion had been so violent.

(IDA gets up and begins gathering her clothing.)

BROWN: Don't get anything on that dress. I have to return it this afternoon.
IDA: Can I not keep it on?
BROWN: You don't need it to leave the hotel. You brought your own clothes, right?
IDA: Yes.

(IDA finishes collecting her clothing and heads toward the bathroom.)

HANNA: You never heard anything else about the little girl, did you?
SALOMON: No.
BROWN: Ida.
(IDA stops right beside SALOMON. SALOMON unconsciously looks in her direction. BROWN shows IDA some blue panties she has left.)

SALOMON: She disappeared without a trace.

(IDA grabs her panties and this time disappears into the bathroom. After a while, the sound of the shower can be heard. BROWN will then get up, wiping himself off with the sheets before getting dressed.)

SALOMON: I spent three days in a Red Cross infirmary. After that, I tried to find her. Believe me, I tried everything, but no one knew anything about her.
HANNA: Not even the teachers or missionaries from the school?
SALOMON: Some of them claimed to know who she was. But you know how priests are with christening every orphaned child with some saint's name... I moved heaven and earth to find out her real name, but to no avail. That little girl came out of nowhere and disappeared in the same way forever.

HANNA: Why did you want to find her? Did you feel responsible?
SALOMON: Of course I did. I wasn't even thirty years old then. If I had just yelled when she stopped in that plaza, she could have come to me and that wouldn't have happened to her.
HANNA: And the photo never would have existed.
SALOMON: Right.
HANNA: And now? Do you regret not helping her?
SALOMON: I haven't asked myself that question for a long time. And you, as a journalist, should know better than to ask.
HANNA: As a journalist, perhaps. But that doesn't stop me from thinking about the little girl.
SALOMON: She couldn't have been fully aware of what was going on. I doubt she even noticed me being there.
HANNA: That may have been the case. But what if she did survive? She would have seen the photo, years later. Don't you think she would have asked that question a thousand times? Why didn't that man help me?
SALOMON: I find that highly improbable.
HANNA: That you would have helped her?
SALOMON: That she's still alive.
HANNA: So you think that she died?
SALOMON: I said it's improbable, not impossible.
HANNA: In that case, if the girl did die, you would have even more reason to have wanted to help her, wouldn't you?
SALOMON: Miss . . . Any moral questions you can ask me on

this, I've already grappled with a thousand times over. It's useless dwelling on what could have been, and how it could have all turned out . . . You can't change the past.

(*Pause.*)

HANNA: What would you do if you found her today?
SALOMON: The girl?
HANNA (*Nodding yes*): Imagine that she is alive, and now a full-grown woman, who is, for example, in one of the rooms of this hotel . . . Imagine that you saw her in the hallway or on the street . . . Do you think that you would recognize her?
SALOMON: I don't know.
HANNA: I would think that you could. You should know her every feature from memory. What would be the first thing you would say to her? Would you ask for forgiveness?
SALOMON: Why? The war wasn't my fault.

(*HANNA's expression turns sour, possibly from not expecting SALOMON to respond as he did. She makes a few notes in her notebook and takes a deep breath.*)

HANNA: It's curious how your life can change in an instant, don't you think? Any given day, a bomb drops near you, or you see a girl leaving a school . . . or someone points a gun at you, and everything changes. Did you ever think about that before?
SALOMON: Before when?

HANNA: Earlier, at the window. When you saw the woman who killed herself.
SALOMON: Sort of.
HANNA: That's got to be difficult for you, keeping in mind what today is. Even *you* commented on it.

(*BROWN, once dressed, opens the window, sits on the window sill, and lights up a cigarette.*)

SALOMON (*Not wanting to continue with the topic*): Aren't we a little off topic for this interview?
HANNA: I'm sorry, it's just that . . . well, you have to understand. You are . . . Frederick Salomon. That says it all. A living legend of photo journalism.
SALOMON: Don't exaggerate.
HANNA: I can't help it. I want to know everything.
SALOMON: No one wants to know everything.
HANNA: I do.
SALOMON: My life has been a lot more boring than some may think. Hell, I'm certain I could learn more things from you than you could from me. And I'm twice your age.
HANNA: Have you ever received death threats?
SALOMON: Yes. Well . . . nothing serious. Anonymous. Lately through e-mail. Some with computer viruses and all.
HANNA: And what do they say?
SALOMON: Nothing. They're stupid. Just ridiculous accusations.

HANNA: For example?

SALOMON: For example what you just said before. How did you put it? "Our people's misfortune was converted into a frivolous symbol of Western guilt."

HANNA: You're not saying that I threatened you, are you?

SALOMON: Hardly. You're not the only person to think that. I have to hear it even in my country. Even from students . . . you know how they are. But the messages usually go a little further.

HANNA: Do they scare you?

SALOMON (*Letting out a chuckle*): No. To scare me, it'd take a little more than four lines scrawled by some fanatic looking for someone to blame. It's one of the consequences of fame: you magically become the scapegoat for the misfortunes of people living halfway round the world.

HANNA: It's normal, I suppose. You've gotten rich from a photo that you took in a country that has known nothing but misery. That may offend people.

SALOMON: Offend is the least of it. People call me a profiteer, a thief, an exploiter...and other more colorful names that I wouldn't want to repeat in front of you. (*HANNA takes down some notes.*)

HANNA: Tell me what a normal day's like in the life of Frederick Salomon.

SALOMON (*Laughing again*): That is really of no interest.

HANNA: Perhaps not for you.

SALOMON: The same as everyone else in the world. I get up, I make breakfast...

HANNA: You live alone.
SALOMON: Yes...
HANNA: What else?
SALOMON: I go to the office, downtown.
HANNA: By car?
SALOMON: Of course.
HANNA: What kind of car do you drive?
SALOMON: It depends. Now it's summer, so a convertible. Do you like cars?
HANNA: I don't really know that much about them. And once you're at the office?
SALOMON: Well, I oversee the magazine.
HANNA: But you're not in photography anymore.
SALOMON: I have a team of expert photographers.
HANNA: But *you* don't pick up a camera.
SALOMON (*Slightly embarrassed*): No.
HANNA: And at the end of the day, you return home. Perhaps you go out to dinner at some trendy restaurant. Or you take in a show and look forward to the next day.
SALOMON: At last you've gotten me to talk about my private life.
HANNA: Well, you had told me that . . .
SALOMON: I already told you that my daily life is pretty boring. I suppose you've gathered enough material for your interview, haven't you? (*Pause. HANNA and SALOMON scrutinize each other.*)
HANNA: Yes. With all my notes and everything you've told

me . . . I'll be able to do it.
SALOMON: Then if you'll excuse me . . . It was a pleasure to meet you.
HANNA: One last thing.
SALOMON: What?
HANNA: I can't believe that *you* didn't think of it. We need some kind of visual for the interview.
SALOMON: Yes, of course. Did you bring a camera?
HANNA: No. I'll make a portrait.
SALOMON: A portrait? You mean a drawing? (*HANNA nods yes as she puts away her notebook and pulls out a large sketch pad and a charcoal drawing pencil.*) They do that a lot at your paper?
HANNA: No. It was my idea. Taking a photograph of the most famous photographer in the world was . . . how should I put it, too easy. And seeing as I'm pretty good with drawing . . .
SALOMON: Will it take long?
HANNA: No. It will just be a sketch. Go ahead and make yourself comfortable and don't move. (*SALOMON begins sitting for HANNA to draw him, though he remains uncertain of the proposition.*) And don't worry, it will come out very well. Photos, perhaps, can't lie, but the charcoal can.
SALOMON: Believe me, so can photographs. (*HANNA begins to draw SALOMON.*)

(*IDA emerges from the bathroom with wet hair and wearing a hotel bathrobe. She carries a plastic bag with the blue dress inside.*)

IDA (*Giving the bag to BROWN*): Here is the dress. You don't shower?
BROWN: I don't need to. I'll start sweating again anyway.
(*BROWN runs his fingers through her hair. IDA wants to pull away from him, but acquiesces.*) Today you really went all out. Your blowjobs are better than some men's . . .
IDA: Did you bring the pills?
BROWN: Of course. I don't like to have debts with anyone. And with you, even less. (*BROWN reaches for his briefcase, opens it, puts in the bag with the dress, and pulls out two pill bottles. He gives the pill bottles to IDA.*) They're the usual. When your daughter's better and back at home, we'll go back to giving her one of the red pills after lunch and two green after dinner. That was the right dosage for her, right?
IDA (*Nodding yes*): They don't take away all the pain, but she can sleep at night and stopped having the cough attacks...
BROWN: Now, what do you say?
IDA: Thank you, Dr. Brown.
BROWN: You know I'm delighted to help you. *(IDA clutches the bottles like they were her most prized possession.)*
IDA: If there is any change. . .I mean, if she wakes up. . .You tell me right away, right?
BROWN: Of course I will.

IDA: I will see you next week then. (*IDA goes toward the closet.*)
BROWN: Wait.

(*SALOMON shifts where he sits.*)

HANNA: Don't move.

(*IDA stops.*)

BROWN: Don't go yet. I have a surprise for you.
IDA: A present?
BROWN: It might be. We'll have to see.
IDA: I don't understand.
BROWN (*Checking his watch*): I'm meeting someone at the reception desk. He's a doctor from the United States, a friend of mine. I've asked him to take a closer look at Sara and her condition.
IDA: He can cure her?
BROWN: Ida, your daughter's illness is incurable. You already know that.
IDA: *Here* it is. But in America . . .
BROWN: *There* also. But with the right treatment she could live a long time, like a normal person. Perhaps your government would take interest in sending her there. It would be a human interest story that might give people around the world a better picture of things.
IDA (*Excited*): My daughter! In America!

BROWN: Slow down there. Before we do anything, my friend has to sign off on it. We have to be certain that Sara can handle the long trip. And that she would make it okay.
IDA: I am sure she will. She is strong.
BROWN: And then we would have to make certain to keep all lines of communication open about her situation. That won't be a problem, I'm sure. The media would kill for a story like this.
IDA: When do you think she will be ready?
BROWN: We'll have to see. If everything goes well, in a few weeks. We have to monitor the coma, see how it progresses. (*Pause.*) You're a very lucky woman, Ida.
IDA: Why did you not tell me all this before?

(*A malicious smile forms on BROWN's face as he begins running his fingers through IDA's hair.*)

BROWN: You're a *very* lucky woman.
IDA: Can I go, too?
BROWN (*Alarmed*): Now? With my friend?
IDA: To America. With Sara.
BROWN: Ah, I don't know. I guess you could. The reporters will want to talk to someone with the main character of the story. And that's you. Do you realize that? If everything turns out well, you'll be in all the papers and on all the TV stations. You'll be famous.
IDA: I don't care about the fame. I only want my daughter to live.
BROWN: Of course you do.

IDA: Why do you do this all for me?
BROWN: That's what the United Nations are for, aren't they? To guarantee democracy, write peace treaties, and help those less fortunate.
IDA: I am serious in wanting to know.
BROWN: You want to save your daughter and I want to save your government, clean up its image a bit. We all end up winning.
IDA: I don't give a shit about our government.
BROWN: Watch yourself with the cuss words. You still haven't mastered our language and you've already got a filthy mouth. . . We'll have to take care of that.

(*SALOMON checks his watch.*)

SALOMON: Is this going to take much longer?
HANNA: No. And don't move.
BROWN: Are you hungry? (*IDA shyly nods her head yes.*) Did you eat breakfast? (*No response from IDA.*) Did you eat dinner last night? (*No response from IDA. BROWN takes out a chocolate candy bar from one of his pockets and gives it to her. She sets the pill bottles next to the book on the nightstand and grabs the candy bar. She distances herself from him as if she fears him taking it from her. She sits on the bed, and devours the chocolate with delight. He comes up behind her and places his hands on her shoulders. She tenses up.*) I won't have that. You have to eat. If you don't eat, you won't have the energy to do anything, and then what good will you be? Don't they pay

you enough at that factory where you're working? (*BROWN begins to casually massage IDA. He pushes aside her hair a little and stares at the scar visible on her back, just at the top of her neck below her hair.*) How in God's name did this happen to you? You never told me what happened. (*IDA looks at her shoulder as if she does not know what BROWN is referring to.*)

IDA: I don't know. I don't remember. (*Pause.*) Can I ask you a question, Dr. Brown?

BROWN: Go ahead.

IDA: Why do you take off your wedding ring when we meet? (*No response from BROWN. He stops massaging her and looks at his left hand.*) Do you feel shame? Or are you afraid that I might rob you it?

BROWN: I do it out of . . . respect.

IDA: Respect.

BROWN: Yes.

IDA: Respect for who? (*No response from BROWN.*) For her, I am certain . . .

BROWN: You think that's silly. (*IDA finishes off the chocolate and angrily crumples the paper.*) You wouldn't understand. I respect what this ring symbolizes. My wife, naturally, but also our marriage, the sacrament, the order . . . Civilization is based on that. On symbols. Our civilization, and yours too, in its own way.

IDA: I thought that you take it off because you love your wife.

BROWN (*Taken aback*): Yes, for that too.

IDA: If I love someone, I would not let him go to the other side of

the world. (*No response from BROWN.*) Do you have children?
BROWN (*Bragging*): Four. Three boys and a girl. My eldest is starting college next year. He says he wants to be a diplomat.
IDA: Are they healthy?
BROWN: Naturally.
IDA: Do you have more chocolate? Sara loves the chocolate.

(*At this moment, the telephone rings. BROWN goes to answer it.*)

(*HANNA finishes drawing.*)

HANNA: Done. You can relax now.
SALOMON: It's about time.
BROWN (*On the phone*): Yes, that's correct.

(*SALOMON and HANNA stand up. He checks his watch.*)

SALOMON: So we're all done now, right?
HANNA: Don't you want to see it?
BROWN (*On the phone*): All right. I'll be right down. (*BROWN hangs up.*)
SALOMON: What?
HANNA: The drawing. I'm sure you've never seen anything like it.
BROWN: My friend just arrived.

SALOMON: That's not necessary.
BROWN: He's waiting for me downstairs.
SALOMON: I trust your talent.
BROWN: Wait for me here. I won't be long.
HANNA: Aren't you the least bit curious? (*SALOMON concedes. HANNA passes SALOMON the sketch pad.*)

(*BROWN grabs some documents from his briefcase and leaves. A restless IDA stays seated on the bed.*)

(*SALOMON looks at the drawing, which makes him noticeably livid.*)

SALOMON: What the fuck is . . .
HANNA: Don't you like it?
SALOMON: How dare you . . . Is this some kind of sick joke?
HANNA: You don't like it? What a disappointment.

SALOMON: Get out of here right now!
HANNA: This after all I've done?
SALOMON: I said, get the hell out of here!
HANNA: What is the problem? You don't see the resemblance? (*Infuriated, SALOMON goes to the telephone and begins to dial. HANNA pulls out her handgun and points it at him. He does not notice the gun.*)
SALOMON (*On the phone*): Yes. Frederick Salomon. (*At this

moment, SALOMON turns and notices that HANNA is pointing the gun at him. He quickly becomes silent.)

(IDA sits up, grabs the book off the table, and thumbs through it.)

HANNA: Hang up right now.
SALOMON (*On the phone*): No, it's nothing . . . No, the room is fine. You don't need to send anyone . . . That won't be necessary, thank you (*SALOMON hangs up. His anger is quickly replaced with fear.*) What the fuck do you think you're doing?
HANNA: What a stupid question. I'm pointing a gun at you.
SALOMON: What do you want?
HANNA: For you to look at my drawing. (*SALOMON, still confused, does not react.*)

(IDA pulls out a photo from between the pages of the book, carefully places it at the head of the bed, and sits by it. The photo is of a little girl.)

HANNA: Look at it! (*SALOMON obeys and looks at it.*)

(IDA caresses the photo tenderly. She begins to hum a lullaby.)

HANNA: And now tell me . . . Do you see the resemblance or not? *(No response from SALOMON. His eyes begin to tear up.)*

SALOMON: Why are you doing this to me?
HANNA: Just answer my question, please. Don't forget that I am the one conducting the interview.
SALOMON (*Bitterly*): Yes, I see the resemblance.
HANNA: People have always said that I was a good judge of faces. I never forget one. You bear a striking similarity, don't you think? Here we always say that daughters resemble their fathers.
SALOMON: How could you do that?
HANNA: I found a picture in your wallet and thought it might be fun.
SALOMON: Fun? That's just . . . grotesque.
HANNA: The hardest part for me was replicating your famous photograph. It's been a while since I saw it. But I think that it came out well enough. It's just a sketch, but I did attend to all the details. I even went as far as to include the title of the book the little girl carried. Did you notice that? (*SALOMON cannot stop staring at the drawing. His eyes display a mixture of disgust, terror, and utter sadness.*) Don't look at it like that. This is your creation. The image that made you famous. The only difference is that the little girl isn't some anonymous person. It's your daughter who's flying through the air with her clothes in flames. It's your daughter looking at you horrified, about to be squashed like a bug. Now doesn't it resemble--oh, how did you put it? "A symbol of peace"? (*SALOMON throws the drawing pad across the room with an audible burst of rage.*)

(*IDA stops humming. She opens the book to a random page and begins to read it out loud in a tender, maternal voice, as if the photograph were really her child in the flesh and blood. She will create different voices for each animal as she reads.*)

IDA: And after traveling for miles and miles, the little pig's balloon landed in the snake's country. "Good day," said the little pig. "Good day," responded the snake, very, very sad.
SALOMON: What do you want from me?
HANNA: Another obvious question, Mr. Salomon.
IDA: "What kind of animal are you?"

(*No response from SALOMON. His voice will break up more and more as he continues.*)

HANNA: I could have killed you earlier. Even before the interview.
IDA: "I am a sssnake," said the snake.
HANNA: But that would have been too easy. And in the end, even senseless. I wanted you to know why you deserved to die. And I wanted to witness it. Perhaps even give you a chance to find . . . whether it's there--a shred of remorse.
IDA: "And why are you so sad?"
HANNA: Or an ounce of shame.
IDA: "Because I don't have any friends. All the other animals are afraid of me," said the snake. And she started to cry.
SALOMON: What side *are* you from? The People's Liberation

Front?
HANNA (*Shaking her head no*): I'm no fanatic.
IDA: "My fangs are full of venom ssso no one will come up to me. But I'm not mean."
SALOMON: I don't think others would agree.
HANNA: Don't insult me.
IDA: "I'm not afraid of you," said the little pig.
SALOMON: You can't kill me.
HANNA: And why not?
IDA: "And why not? You have to be afraid of me."
SALOMON: They'll hear the gunshot.
IDA: "Your skin is beautiful and very colorful," responded the little pig.
HANNA: In this city, people no longer hear gunshots.
IDA: "It's not your fault that your fangs are full of venom."
SALOMON: Everyone in the hotel knows you are with me. We came in together.
IDA: "And if you cry so bitterly, you can't be so mean," he added.
HANNA: I'm a respected journalist from the official newspaper of the regime. It seems like you've forgotten that. This morning I sang our national anthem with my colleagues at work and this afternoon I'll be in a state of shock for having been the last person to see you alive.
IDA: The snake looked at the little pig with her big snake eyes filled with tears. And the little pig felt sorry for her. "Can I pet you," he asked?
SALOMON: No . . .you wouldn't...

IDA: "Of courssse you can," she whispered with a smile.

HANNA: I most certainly would.

IDA: The little pig, little by little, got closer and closer and ran his little hoof along the snake's scales. "Your skin is very soft. I didn't expect that," he exclaimed, surprised.

SALOMON: There's money in my wallet. Foreign currency. Take it.

HANNA: How much are you offering me?

SALOMON: Everything that's there. There's about five hundred dollars.

IDA: "If you're not happy here, you can travel with me in my balloon," said the little pig.

HANNA: Is that the price you put on your life? Five hundred miserable dollars?

IDA: But the snake, instead of responding, opened her big snake mouth, showed her big snake fangs and . . . chomp! She tried to bite him.

SALOMON: Take my credit cards too if you want.

IDA: The little pig stepped back, frightened. Luckily, the snake didn't harm him. "Why did you do that?"

SALOMON: Why are you doing this to me?

IDA: The snake started to cry again, and while slithering back into her little hole, she said in her little snake voice: "Now do you undersssstand why I'm ssso sssad?"

HANNA: I'm doing you a favor, Mr. Salomon.

(*IDA closes the book.*)

IDA (*To the photo, whispering in her own voice*): Now do you understand why I'm so sad?

HANNA: You should be thanking me. Not everyone is given the opportunity to die in a way that . . . comes full circle.

SALOMON: What do you mean?

HANNA: Just think about it. After twenty years, you return to the country that gave meaning to your life only now to have it taken away . . . And precisely today, the anniversary of your daughter's death. Don't you find that appropriate? (*No response from SALOMON.*)

(*IDA lies down on the bed, gazing at the photograph.*)

HANNA: I hope that before coming you had time to take flowers to her grave. (*SALOMON breaks down crying.*)

SALOMON: Please . . . Let me go. I swear I won't tell a soul. Please, please . . .

HANNA: Please . . . stop begging and whining like a child. I detest that in a man.

SALOMON: I'll do whatever you want.

HANNA: Whatever I want? (*SALOMON nods his head. HANNA thinks it over.*) Good, because there is something I want you to do.

SALOMON: What?

HANNA: Just answer one question. If your answer is correct, I'll let you go. If not, I'll shoot.

SALOMON: That's it?

HANNA: It's that easy.
SALOMON: It sounds . . . a little savage.
HANNA: I don't think you have any other option. (*A pause as SALOMON thinks it over.*)
SALOMON: All right. What's the question?

(*Pause. HANNA takes great care in articulating her question.*)

HANNA: What is my name?
SALOMON: What?
HANNA: What is my name? Just tell me my name.
SALOMON: That's the question?
HANNA: Yes, and it's not very complicated, keeping in mind that we just met a little over a half hour ago (*SALOMON struggles to remember.*) You don't remember? Just my first name will be enough. (*SALOMON feels totally helpless having no recollection of her name.*)
SALOMON: I'm sorry, I. . . .
HANNA: You don't remember. And do you give a shit? Well, now you do, that's for sure. Now that your life depends on it.
SALOMON: Please . . .
HANNA: Hanna. My name is Hanna.
SALOMON: Hanna.
HANNA: I'm sorry.
SALOMON: Don't shoot.
HANNA: Give me a reason not to.
SALOMON: I've never done anything to you.

HANNA: Oh yes you have.

SALOMON: I have? To you?

HANNA: You still haven't figured it out? *(SALOMON becomes speechless as his voice suffocates from crying.)* Take a good look at me and concentrate. Don't you remember my face? *(A confused SALOMON shakes his head no.)* The girl in the photo, Mr. Salomon. That's me. *(SALOMON's face turns white as surprise and doubt overtake his mind. His mouth agape, a speechless SALOMON covers his mouth with his hand. HANNA smiles with an air of false innocence. At that very moment, someone knocks on the door. He jumps and checks his watch.)*

SALOMON: That's . . . It should be . . . From the committee, they've come to get me.

HANNA: Get rid of them.

SALOMON: How can I? I'm having lunch with these people . . . There's the ceremony . . .

(There is another insistent knock at the door. HANNA tries to keep her voice down.)

HANNA: Fuck the ceremony! Make something up. *(HANNA goes toward the bathroom.)* And don't do anything stupid. I'll be listening to you.

(HANNA closes herself in the bathroom. Another knock at the door. SALOMON wipes the tears from his eyes, takes a deep

breath, and opens the door. BROWN enters without the papers he had left with earlier.)

BROWN: Fred, my boy.
SALOMON (*Pretending everything is okay*): How are you doing? (*SALOMON and BROWN hug and continue on like two old buddies with more in common than they care to remember.*)

BROWN: What's taking so long . . . (*Slightly concerned.*) Have you been crying?
SALOMON (*Shaking his head no*): It's just . . .allergies.
BROWN (*Not buying it, but tactful*): Yeah, right. Look, I really appreciate your coming. I speak for the committee and myself. I know that it can't be easy . . .
SALOMON: Spare me the speech, okay?
BROWN (*Going to the minibar*): Fine. Do you like this suite I got you?
SALOMON: It's perfect. Thank you.
BROWN: Is there anymore whiskey or did you drink it all already? (*Seeing the plastic cup.*) Well . . . I see your habits haven't changed. (*BROWN pours himself a generous portion of whisky into one of the glasses. BROWN notices SALOMON's gloves. Joking.*) Still afraid to reach out and touch someone, Fred?

(*SALOMON does not laugh, having not found the joke funny. BROWN recognizes SALOMON's discomfort.*)

SALOMON: How's Gladys?
BROWN: Same as always. Getting fatter. One of these days she'll explode.
SALOMON: You should be there for her more.
BROWN: Nah, she's already got herself a golf instructor. (*SALOMON wipes the sweat from his forehead with his handkerchief.*) Are you feeling all right?
SALOMON: What? No. Yes. It's the . . . this heat. And I'm nervous . . .with all of this.
BROWN: It's this country that's making you feel bad. You and everybody else. The World Health Organization should place a ban on this place.
SALOMON (*Not finding the joke funny*): Listen.
BROWN: Shouldn't you get changed for lunch?
SALOMON: I'm afraid that I'm not going to be able to make it.
BROWN (*Laughing*): You and your jokes.
SALOMON: I'm not joking.
BROWN: Aw, c'mon, don't be stupid. Clean yourself up a bit and let's go.
SALOMON: I said no.

(*Pause. The smile disappears from BROWN's face.*)

BROWN: What am I missing?
SALOMON: Nothing. I have . . . some business to attend to.
BROWN: And this "business" can't wait?
SALOMON: No.

BROWN: Let's see if I understand. You've been here less than an hour and you've already got some other commitment more important than having lunch with the Minister of Tourism and Communication? And let's not forget the ambassadors from fifteen of the world's most powerful nations.
SALOMON: Basically, yes.

(*BROWN walks around the room observing every detail. Finally, BROWN focuses on the bed where IDA is lying and nods with a smile.*)

BROWN: What's her name?
SALOMON: What?
BROWN: It's a woman, right?

(*SALOMON's attention turns to the bathroom door, panicked by the direction of the conversation.*)

SALOMON: How . . . ? I . . . No . . .

(*BROWN approaches HANNA's bag and grabs it, as if it were a clue from a crime scene.*)

BROWN: C'mon, it takes a little more to fool Dr. Brown. Who is she? A prostitute? A lover from twenty years ago?
SALOMON: Look, don't . . .
BROWN: You waste no time. Where do you have her? In the

bathroom? No . . . You're more traditional. You must have hid her in the closet.

SALOMON: You don't understand.

BROWN (S*uddenly flying off the handle and resorting to curses for the first time*): No. It's *you* who don't understand. The United Nations spent more organizing this goddamn lunch than to write up the peace treaty. This lunch is the first sign of this country westernizing after half a century of hostility. At this lunch, my friend, they'll decide on more policies than at the fucking Yalta Conference. And you can't throw it all to shit because some two-penny whore hasn't finished you off yet.

SALOMON: I'm sure you can come up with some excuse . . .

BROWN: We've already got an excuse. The excuse is your fucking award, it's a ploy to get the desperate masses to tune in to their televisions. That's why we need you. Just for that. For you to show up, gorge yourself on seafood, and give an emotional little speech on human rights. That's all. I don't think that's asking for too much.

SALOMON: I'm asking you as a personal favor.

BROWN: You're not in a position to ask for favors.

SALOMON: Look, we're friends.

BROWN: Exactly. And I hope that doesn't change. But is this how you pay me for everything I've done for you? *(No response from SALOMON.)* I've been able to get you back in the limelight. Even though you may not deserve it, you're a star again.

SALOMON: Or better said, a puppet.

BROWN: Big deal. You've already been that for twenty years. Your photo was the one with fire. Why do you think you *had* such unprecedented mass exposure?
SALOMON: Either way . . .
BROWN: Don't go complaining, Fred. Being a puppet--as you put it--saved your life. Since then, you've been living pretty comfortably. And what have you done for the greater good of man in all this time? I'll tell you: nothing. You sit and rot in an office filled with all the modern amenities while you go on living your life in the past. Then you cry alone off somewhere in the corner whining and asking, "Why is life so unfair? Why did this all have to happen to me?" It's no wonder your wife . . . (*Pause.*) Sorry if I'm being too harsh, but I've got a lot at stake here. And so do you. (*No response from SALOMON. BROWN finishes his whisky.*) An hour from now, I want to see you at the Presidential Palace. You're not gonna waste anymore of my time. You take care of your own . . . "business." (*BROWN goes to leave. Flippant.*) One last thing. Whatever you do with this woman, just make sure she doesn't go and kill herself or something.
SALOMON: What?
BROWN: A little while ago some local prostitute threw herself from one of the hotel windows.
SALOMON: I already saw that.
BROWN: It won't take much to keep your affairs under wraps. But you watch yourself. We can't go having any kind of scandal here. (*SALOMON nods his head in defeat. BROWN*

continues with confidence.) Fred. Don't let me down, okay? For old time's sake.
SALOMON (*In a barely audible voice*): For old time's...

(*BROWN opens the door and exits. HANNA immediately comes out from the bathroom, still holding the gun, but not pointing it. She relaxes and cradles the gun like a rag doll. They both stare at each other defiantly for a while.*)

HANNA: For a while I thought that you were going to leave with him. Why didn't you? Out there they're waiting for you with cameras, praise, prestige . . (*Without a word, SALOMON studies HANNA's every move and sound.*) Ah, that's it . . . Curiosity. What a bad vice . . . You should know that old saying: curiosity killed the cameraman.
SALOMON: You don't want to shoot me anymore?
HANNA: I don't know. Your conversation with your friend made me think it over. My life has been pretty shitty, I assure you, but your life . . .

(*BROWN enters carrying the same papers he had left with earlier. IDA places the photo in the book and sits up on the bed.*)

BROWN: Sorry I took so long. I ran into someone that I hadn't seen in a while.
SALOMON: He talks too much.

IDA: What did he say to you? How did it go?
BROWN: I showed him Sara's medical records and . . . well, he said there is a possibility that she'll come out of it.
(IDA places her hands on her cheeks with delighted surprise, unable to believe the news.)

HANNA: I don't know which one of us lost more in that explosion. In all this time, I've gotten along okay.
BROWN: This afternoon he'll stop by the hospital and do a check up.
HANNA: I was lucky. I could study and move forward in a world that was being destroyed.
IDA: And when will they take her to America?
BROWN: We'll have to see.
HANNA: But you, on the other hand . . . You've been living in the "New World", heaven on earth, the birthplace of democracy, and the land of opportunity . . . but you didn't know how to reap its benefits. You've just been a miserable wretch for the past twenty years.
BROWN: Once there, they predict her treatment will last a month, month and a half until she can leave the hospital.
HANNA: Take off the gloves.
IDA: And then?
SALOMON: What?
BROWN: And then what?

(HANNA points the gun at SALOMON.)

HANNA: I said, take off the gloves.

(*Slightly flustered, SALOMON takes off his gloves. His hands are healthy, showing no signs of eczema.*)

IDA: And when she's better . . . they'll return her back to us here?
BROWN: Of course not. Then they'll enroll the girl in a school, and for you they'll find you a suitable job and you'll be able to buy all the chocolate candy bars you want.
HANNA: Now give them to me.

(*Overcome with emotion, IDA throws her arms around BROWN's neck and hugs him.*)

(*SALOMON gives HANNA the gloves. Without the gloves, he becomes noticeably self-conscious, uncertain what to do with his hands. She stops pointing the gun at him.*)

IDA: Oh, Dr. Brown, thank you, thank you...
HANNA: Thank you.
BROWN: You're welcome. But there is still one small detail that we need to work out.
IDA: What is this?
BROWN: The payment.

(*HANNA casually sniffs the gloves, finding that she likes the smell. She sets the gloves aside.)*

IDA: What payment?

BROWN: Don't play innocent with me thinking that all of this is gonna come for free. (*IDA backs away, her smile quickly erased from her face.)*
HANNA: So how do you feel now?
IDA: You know I don't have any money.
BROWN: Who said anything about money? Have you paid me with money up till now? (*IDA understands, steps up closer, and starts to undo BROWN's pants. He stops her.)*
SALOMON: What do you want? To humiliate me? (*HANNA laughs with apparent sincerity, completely lacking hostility.)*
BROWN: No. This time a quick blowjob isn't enough. For half a dozen pills, perhaps, but now this is a serious business.
HANNA: Your idea of humiliation is truly curious.
BROWN: You wouldn't believe how expensive airline tickets have gotten recently.
IDA: What do you want me to do?

(***BROWN** smiles maliciously. He goes to his briefcase, puts his papers away, and pulls out a long cord. While speaking he slowly wraps the cord around his hand with a look of intimidation.)*

HANNA: I pity you, you know? So I don't think I'm going to kill you, even though that may be best for you.

SALOMON: Then what *do* you want?

HANNA: I'm still not certain. (*Adopting SALOMON's tone from the beginning.*) Please, make yourself comfortable. We'll think of something soon enough. (*SALOMON makes himself comfortable. HANNA pulls out a pack of cigarettes and lights one up.*)

BROWN: For starters, you'll get in the bathtub and let me piss all over you. If I say open your mouth, you'll open your mouth. If I say swallow, you'll swallow. Then we'll go to the bed and I'm going to tie you up. I'm not exactly sure how. I like to improvise. The only thing I am certain of is that you won't be able to move. I'll be in charge of that. Then I'll penetrate you in your vagina and then your anus. Right now, I recommend that you relax. I left the Vaseline at home and if you're tense... well, we wouldn't want to do any more harm than necessary. I'll gag your mouth with something. We'll see what. If I remove it, it'll be for you to lick, not for you to talk. Have I made myself clear? No talking. Not a word. And especially no cuss words. You already know that I don't like those. You can, however, cry, if you like. Tears excite me. If you cry, it will be simply . . . perfect. Do you have any questions?

(*IDA is frozen almost lifeless without expression.
Automatically, her head shakes no as she undoes the belt from her bathrobe.*)

BROWN: Shall we begin? (*BROWN grabs the curtains that separate the sitting room from the bedroom and closes them forcefully. The sounds of the metal rings on the bar signal that of a death sentence. At the same moment, a more ear-shattering sound is heard from outside, like that of a thunder crash or mountain collapsing.*)

(*SALOMON reacts suddenly to the noise. HANNA stays calm.*)

SALOMON: What was that?
HANNA: I'm sure it was just a building collapsing. It happens a lot. The war has scarred and weakened them too much. (*SALOMON instinctively looks at the walls of room.*) Don't worry about the hotel. It's not going to fall. Guess who stayed here during the war. (*Pause.*) Don't you want to ask me any questions?
SALOMON: I thought that *you* were conducting the interview.
HANNA: Come on, I know you're dying to know.
SALOMON: You're wrong.
HANNA: You've been looking for me for twenty years and now you have the balls to tell me that you don't have any questions for me?
SALOMON: Exactly.
HANNA: And why, if I may ask?
SALOMON: Because I don't think that you are the girl in the photo.
HANNA: You don't think I am.

SALOMON (*Nodding yes*): I don't believe a single word you've told me today. I'm certain you're just some . . .fanatic looking for attention.

HANNA: Please, don't be insulting.

SALOMON: I'm sorry, but that is what I believe.

HANNA: Then why didn't you run out of here earlier when you had the chance?

(*A pause as SALOMON thinks up a response.*)

SALOMON: Show it to me. I want proof.

HANNA: I give you my word and you don't trust me?

SALOMON: I suppose I have to trust in someone who's been threatening me with a weapon?

(*Now HANNA thinks over her response.*)

SALOMON: We've come full circle. That's what you said. If you're going to kill me, don't you think that you should assure me that you're the right person? That was your plan, right? Then let's go with it. You come full circle now, and convince me.

(*After reflecting for a moment, HANNA stands in front of SALOMON, setting the gun aside, and begins to unbutton her blouse slowly. Once unfastened, she turns and lowers her shirt to show him her back. She pulls aside her hair with one hand.*)

We see HANNA's back, neck, and part of her scalp which are covered in a large scar from a severe burn. HANNA holds still as SALOMON, seated and expressionless, looks at her. At one given moment, he gets up and approaches her. Missing his gloves, his hands tremble when he holds his hands right over her shoulders, hesitating to touch her. With a deep breath and with the expression of finally coming home after a long journey, he touches his fingers to the scar. Slowly, he traces the outline of her deformed, burned skin. After a moment, SALOMON yanks his hands away as if expecting punishment for committing a dirty deed. He takes a step back and notices that the gun is close enough for him to grab and be able to save his life. HANNA turns and buttons up her blouse. They both look at each other and then at the gun, from which they are the same distance. Neither go for the gun. Instead, SALOMON moves away from her, looking at his hands while HANNA finishes buttoning her shirt.)

HANNA: Now do you believe me?
SALOMON: No.
HANNA: Well. I didn't think I would need more conclusive proof.
SALOMON: You'll have to try harder. You're not the only girl in this country with her skin burned.
HANNA: Clearly not. But don't you find it coincidental that my marks match those of the burning girl in the photograph?
SALOMON: No one said anything about coincidences.

HANNA: What are you insinuating?
SALOMON: You wouldn't believe the number of women who have come forth insisting that they are her. Some said the flames never scorched their skin, or that with the passage of time their wounds disappeared. But others . . .
HANNA: Did it to themselves?
SALOMON: There are people prepared to do whatever it takes for money, fame, or, simply, to move to the "Western World."
HANNA: Those women are sick.
SALOMON: There were even mothers those first few years . . . They brought me their little girls . . . .deformed by the flames. . .
HANNA: I am not like that.
SALOMON: I'm not sure of that.
HANNA: But how could you think that I would. . .
SALOMON: I already said it wouldn't be the first time.
HANNA: I have endured this . . . atrocity . . . my whole life. You have no idea what it's like. Sometimes it still gives me trouble. Even after all of this time . . .
SALOMON: I am truly sorry, but you are an imposter until you can prove otherwise. An imposter as well as crazy, just like all the others.
HANNA: The others wanted to take advantage of you with their lies. I haven't asked you for anything.
SALOMON: No. You only want to kill me. (*HANNA takes a brief glance at the gun, abandoned like a worthless penny.*) And perhaps you still want to. But don't think that I'll make this any easier for you than I did for all the others.

HANNA: Fine. Then ask me. Ask me something that only I could know.
SALOMON: What's the use in that? I'm sure you've studied all the literature published on my photograph. You should know what happened even better than I would.
HANNA: There must have been something that was never made public. Some detail that you held back for yourself, just for when this moment would arrive. I'm certain of it.
SALOMON: Perhaps, I have.
HANNA: I'm certain of it.

(SALOMON pauses to think. He goes to the minibar and pours himself another whisky. After touching things, he wipes his hands on his pants, as if wiping away some invisible filth.)

SALOMON: How old were you then?
HANNA: Seven.
SALOMON: Do you remember many things from that day?
HANNA: Some. A few. The least important, I suppose. Small details. I'll be honest with you, there are things that I don't know exactly if they're memories, or imaginations, or images that came to me later, when I read your books . . . All together it's a little fuzzy . . .
SALOMON: A little fuzzy . . . That's a good way to cover your ass in case you make a mistake.
HANNA: That morning for breakfast I had a glass of milk and a

banana. I remember it perfectly well because it had been months since I had had fruit.

SALOMON: That's not helping any.

HANNA: All day, a strong wind was blowing, from the north I think it was.

SALOMON: That's normal for that time of year. Please be more specific.

HANNA: Well, I don't know what you are expecting to hear.

SALOMON: Take, for example, why no one knew anything about you. The missionaries, the teachers at the school. Why didn't they recognize you when I showed them the photograph?

HANNA: That wasn't my school.

SALOMON: Oh, it wasn't? Then which was your school?

HANNA: The orphanage, run by the Piarist nuns. It was right by. You have to remember. Before you get to the central market.

SALOMON: That's convenient.

HANNA: What do you mean?

SALOMON: That orphanage was destroyed when the city fell and, as I'm sure you know, not a single nun was left alive, and much less a virgin, when the rebels occupied it. No other account could corroborate your story.

HANNA: It's the truth.

SALOMON: Then you must have been grateful.

HANNA: I don't see why.

SALOMON: If that bomb hadn't been dropped near you, you would have returned to the orphanage you say you studied at and you would have been raped, mutilated, and murdered at the

hands of merciless guerillas. *(No response from HANNA.)* If that wasn't your school, then what were you doing there?
HANNA: After class, I went to look for a friend of mine. She studied there.
SALOMON: What was her name?
HANNA: Ida.
SALOMON: Ida what?
HANNA: I don't know.
SALOMON: Ida is a common name here. What did the missionaries call her?
HANNA: I don't know.
SALOMON: Didn't you say that you were friends? You should know her name.
HANNA: I told you I don't know, dammit! Her name was Ida. Just Ida!

(*Pause.*)

SALOMON: Why did you go to see her?
HANNA: I had to give her a book.
SALOMON: What book?
HANNA: A story book. The one that's in the photo.
SALOMON: And you decided to meet at the school?
HANNA: Yes.
SALOMON: And why not at her house? Or at the orphanage?
HANNA: I don't know.
SALOMON: Maybe your classes ended before hers.

HANNA: I don't know. Maybe so. I don't remember.
SALOMON: You didn't hear the sirens?
HANNA: Yes, but I was distracted.
SALOMON: Why?
HANNA: I was on the toilet.
SALOMON: And your friend didn't wait for you?
HANNA: You already know that she didn't.
SALOMON: And you never saw her again?
HANNA: No.
SALOMON: You were such close friends . . . Didn't she go see you at the hospital afterwards?
HANNA: I never said that they took me to the hospital.
SALOMON: Where did they take you then?
HANNA: I don't know.
SALOMON: Of course. You don't know that either.
HANNA: What do you want from me?
SALOMON: Only for you to remember what you can.
HANNA: Do you think I have a photographic memory?
SALOMON: I think that you're making it all up. The only thing you've offered are accounts that would be impossible to substantiate. What I want are facts. Concrete facts. What happened afterwards. Where you went. Who knew you.
HANNA: The first memories I had after the explosion were when I was ten or eleven years old.
SALOMON: Once again, very convenient. Shock-induced amnesia always helps, eh?
HANNA: They told me that I was taken to the southern mountains

before the city fell. That's all I know. That's where I grew up and studied, and I didn't return here until I was older. It was then when I saw that fucking picture for the first time.

(*Pause. SALOMON checks his watch.*)

SALOMON: This is starting to bore me. I've already heard this too many times.

(*HANNA changes gears and looks at the gun. SALOMON also looks at the gun. They both concentrate on the gun as if it were secretly whispering into their ears.*)

HANNA: Fine, I guess you're right. It's all lies. So then why would I come back to kill you?
SALOMON: Maybe you only wanted to make me think you were going to kill me.
HANNA: That would be a little contrived, don't you think?
SALOMON: Then why haven't you done it?
HANNA: And why haven't *you* done it? (*HANNA and SALOMON look at each other suspiciously. He downs the whisky.*)
SALOMON: Let's go back to the explosion for a moment.
HANNA: What do you want to know?
SALOMON: You were in the bathroom and you heard the sirens. What did you do?
HANNA: It scared me, so I ran out as fast as I could.
SALOMON: Not possible. The planes hadn't arrived yet.

HANNA: I was sidetracked. I went back inside.
SALOMON: Why?
HANNA: I had left the book. I realized right before getting out to the street.
SALOMON: They were about to bombard the city and all you could think about was a book?
HANNA: It was Ida's book, my friend's. I couldn't lose it.
SALOMON: That's all you had.
HANNA: That's all I have. I run up the stairs. I don't see anyone. Everyone's gone. I go into the bathroom, but I can't find the book. I don't understand why until I realize that I'm on the wrong floor. It's then that I hear the planes. (*It seems that HANNA is forcing herself to remember. As she continues to speak, her own words begin to affect her more and more.*)
SALOMON: Go on.
HANNA: The book is on the top floor. I grab it and run for the stairs. I'm going down three steps at a time. I stumble and fall. My knee hurts and starts to bleed, but I don't cry. I hear the engines from the bombers overhead. The glass from the windows rattles. Something must have exploded near by. I get up. My leg hurts, but I keep going. I get to the entryway. I'm afraid. The sound of the planes is so loud that it's as if they've invaded the building and are chasing me like a pack of wild dogs. Another explosion. The rafters are creaking and dust falls from the ceiling. All I can think is run, run, run . . . I leave the school. The plaza is deserted. I can't get any air. Maybe from exhaustion, or panic, I don't know . . . I look all around

me. All the buildings look the same. I can't find the bomb shelter. I stop. I try to look for someone, something to tell me "Come, Hanna, it's over here!" But I don't see anything, I don't see anyone. The only thing I'm thinking is, "you have to save yourself," but my feet are stuck to the ground. And I look overhead. I remember it all too well. I look up into the sky and I see them. Buzzing around through the clouds like vultures. Their eyes beating down on me. And all of a sudden . . . (*HANNA stops, unable to continue, as if the memories have transported her into a dreamland.*)

(*An agonizing screech from IDA emanates from behind the curtains. This cry of excruciating pain shatters the air before it is drowned out by a muffled cry.*)

(*SALOMON remains absorbed in HANNA's narrative.*)

SALOMON: And all of a sudden?
HANNA: I can't remember anything else after that moment. Only these permanent dreamlike impressions. A brutal silence and a single loud note so sharp and mind shattering. And darkness . . .
SALOMON: Nothing else?
HANNA: I don't know.
SALOMON: Did you see me?
HANNA: I don't know!
SALOMON: I was there. Did you see me when you were flying through the air, Hanna?

HANNA: I don't know! I don't know!
SALOMON: Of course you did. You saw me. It was only a millisecond, but you saw me. Pointing the camera at you.
HANNA: The camera . . . A dark black shiny eye . . . watching me.
SALOMON: And what else?
HANNA: It's only a dream . . .
SALOMON: And what else!
HANNA: A shirt, a jacket, maybe.
SALOMON: A jacket. What color?
HANNA: I don't know.
SALOMON: Yes, you do.
HANNA: Yellow?
SALOMON: Yellow.
HANNA: And something else.
SALOMON: What?
HANNA: Some other color.
SALOMON: Red?
HANNA: Yes.
SALOMON: Where?
HANNA: Blood?
SALOMON: I asked you where.
HANNA: On your arm?
SALOMON: An armband.
HANNA: An armband.
SALOMON: A white armband with the word "Press" written in red letters.

(*A long pause.*)

(*BROWN slowly opens the curtains. He is half dressed, sweaty, but visibly satisfied. On the bed, IDA, dejected and depleted, lies completely naked with her hands tied behind her back. The rope is also wrapped around her neck. Her eyes are open, focused on nothing, concentrating only on loathing and breathing. She remains motionless. BROWN lights a cigarette and observes IDA like a painter would one of his paintings after having finished the last stroke.*)

SALOMON (*In a barely audible voice*): Hanna . . . (*No response from HANNA, as if no one had called her name. SALOMON looks at her, not knowing whether to be fascinated, surprised, or fearful.*) You could be . . .
HANNA: Do you believe me now?
SALOMON: It really could be you . . . Look me in the eyes. (*HANNA looks at SALOMON.*) Why did you wait so long? Why didn't you say anything before?
HANNA: You would have thought me crazy.
SALOMON: Do you realize what this means, if it's really you?
HANNA (*Nodding yes*): That I have every right in the world to hate you.
SALOMON: So do I, Hanna. So do I. (*With that said, SALOMON approaches the sketch pad with HANNA's drawing and picks it up. He looks at it as if addressing the picture and not her.*) Today. Precisely today. (*SALOMON passes his hand over the*

drawing.) A miserable wretch who doesn't know how to reap the benefits from the land of opportunity. Isn't that what you said? Twenty years ago, I lost you. And since then . . .fear, only fear. And the image. Always the image. That goddamn image. (*Pause.* SALOMON *takes a deep breath and looks at* HANNA. *He then looks at the drawing and continues to address it.*) There came a time when I no longer wanted to see it. I didn't want to see you. In your eyes I saw terror, surprise, sadness . . . You watched me watching you at the brink of death, and I saw it all. But most of all contempt. Contempt for me, for us, for all those with the indecency to go on living. Complete and utter contempt. That is what you made me feel. You. (*Looking at HANNA.*) Her. (*Pause.*) (*Referring to the drawing.*) She died without me, while I was trying to find you. She died in that Western palette of pastels. What's the use of living in paradise if you can't save the life of your own child? My wife didn't know how to forgive me. There was nothing to forgive, but she didn't know that. She just needed someone to blame, and so did I. (*Pause.*) I hid all the copies I had. All of them. The original print, the magazine covers I had so proudly framed . . . I hid them all in the attic. And can you believe that I haven't gone back up into the attic in years?

(*BROWN puts out his cigarette and begins to untie IDA with a paternal tenderness. She allows him to do so without a fuss. The cord has left deep marks in her skin.*)

SALOMON (*Continues*): But that didn't stop me from seeing you. You. Her. It's all the same. I couldn't stop seeing you. You were everywhere: on the television, on the street, in magazines, gift shops, fast-food restaurants . . . When I thought that I could finally begin to forget you, your eyes came back to haunt me even in the most unsuspecting of places. Always keeping close watch over every last corner of the city. From any city in the world. I would have given anything to erase those eyes. To erase them from my mind forever. I was also a victim. Being from a Western nation doesn't protect you from a world full of disaster, death, and desperation . . . from *my* world. (*SALOMON sets the sketch pad next to the gun. He picks up the gun, approaches HANNA, and points the gun at her.*) I never would have thought that things would end this way, that I would be capable of doing . . .what I'm just about to do.

(*The words frighten HANNA but she contains her fear while remaining motionless. It looks like SALOMON is about to shoot, but he does not. Instead, he turns his hand and offers the gun to her. She lets out a sigh of relief and takes the gun.*)

BROWN: You were fantastic, Ida. I don't understand why you don't do this professionally. You could make a good living at this. (*BROWN has finished untying IDA and has started to get dressed. She sits up and covers herself with the bathrobe. She avoids touching her own skin as if it were covered in filth.*)

SALOMON: Come with me.

HANNA: Where?

SALOMON: There are a ton of people who'll want to meet you. They'll want to hear your story and feel the same emotions they lived through twenty years ago.

HANNA: That's not what I was looking for.

SALOMON: Neither was I. But we don't have any other choice. We can't change the past. Let's forget it. It doesn't matter who I was and who you were. Starting now, we can become whoever we want to be. (*No response from HANNA.*) Do you understand what I'm saying?

HANNA (*Nodding yes*): And if I refuse?

SALOMON: You won't.

(*IDA has remained seated on the bed, without any reaction.*)

BROWN: Don't just sit there. Get dressed. We have to leave this room before noon.

SALOMON: You won't even believe everything that's waiting for you out there.

BROWN: They've got new guests coming.

(*SALOMON extends a handshake to HANNA. She hesitates, but accepts. They shake hands and smile.*)

BROWN (*Continues*): Did you hear me?

(*IDA tentatively turns toward BROWN, as if his voice had been muffled or she was not certain that she had heard him.*)

IDA: What?
BROWN: You have five minutes to leave the room.
HANNA: Your hands are soft. I didn't expect that.

(*SALOMON releases the handshake and goes to the telephone. He picks up the phone and dials.*)

(*BROWN is all dressed and places the cord in his briefcase.*)

SALOMON (*On the phone*): This is Fred . . . Are you already at the presidential palace? . . . Yes, of course I'll show up on time. Count me in and have them set another place at the table. I'm bringing a very special guest . . . I'm certain you'll all be delighted to meet her . . . You'll see soon enough . . . I want to be in the limelight again, my friend . . . Yes, I'll see you soon. (*SALOMON hangs up.*) Get your things. Your government has invited you to lunch. (*HANNA places the gun and sketch pad in her bag.*)
BROWN: Ida, did you hear me? (*No response from IDA.*) Look, you're gonna go one way or another. If you want them to throw you out on the street that's your decision. (*BROWN grabs his briefcase and goes to leave.*)
HANNA: Shouldn't we go?

IDA: Dr. Brown.
SALOMON: Go ahead on down and wait for me at the front desk. I have to take care of something.
BROWN: What?
HANNA: All right. (*HANNA goes to leave.*)
IDA: Are you going to the hospital?
BROWN: When? Now?
SALOMON: Hanna, wait.

(*HANNA stops next to BROWN.*)

IDA: Now, this afternoon, whenever.
BROWN: Why do you want to know?

(IDA slowly gets up to grab the book off the nightstand and gives it to BROWN.)

SALOMON: When you tell your story to the Minister and the ambassadors . . . don't say that you looked up into the sky while you were in the middle of the plaza. The little girl never did that. And my jacket was white. Not yellow. *(HANNA gives SALOMON a hard stare.)* We wouldn't want anyone to think you were an imposter, now would we?
HANNA: No, of course not.
SALOMON: Go ahead then. I'll be right down.

(HANNA allows a half smile to escape, she opens the door and

exits.)

(BROWN looks at the book that IDA has given to him.)

IDA: This is Sara's book. You can give it to a nurse, right? It is the last favor that I ask you. *(SALOMON finds his gloves, he goes to put them on, but rethinks it, and leaves them aside.)* Most important you must imitate the animals. If you do not talk like the animals, the story is not funny. *(BROWN tosses away the book onto the bed.)* What do you do?

BROWN: Ida, your daughter died late last night. *(No response from IDA. BROWN's words have opened a floodgate of pain that extinguishes all hope.)* I'm very sorry. *(With that said, BROWN exits. Utterly crushed, IDA freezes, like a pillar of salt, attempting to process his words.)*

(SALOMON puts on his jacket and goes to the window. He places his hands on the windowsill, takes a deep breath, and looks down below.)

(IDA suddenly reacts by running to the phone, picking it up, and dialing.)

IDA *(On the phone with a barely audible voice)*: Hello. Is this Hospital of the Republic? . . . I call to know about . . . The patient in room 161 . . . Yes. Intensive Care . . . How . . . How is she? . . . Her mother . . . Ida **. . .** *(She is about to give* *her last name but is cut off.*) Yes, I wait. (*The wait feels like an eternity. IDA holds onto one last shred of hope that BROWN was misinformed about her daughter.*) Yes, I am still here.

(*As she listens, IDA becomes crestfallen. She opens her mouth to scream but emits no sound, only she can hear the scream in her head. With no response, she hangs up. The click from the headset landing in the cradle sounds out her sentence. Slowly and unable to cry, IDA goes to the night table and grabs the pill bottles. She sits on the bed and, as before, clutches onto the bottles like they were her most prized possession. IDA then picks up the storybook and ceremoniously tucks the storybook in under the covers as if putting her child to rest.*)

(*SALOMON pulls away from the window and when he turns, something he had not seen before on the bed grabs his attention. At this moment, it seems that SALOMON and IDA cross glances. SALOMON approaches the bed and pulls out the storybook tucked in under the covers. Upon reading the title, SALOMON chokes up, recognizing and remembering the title. Right after, he turns to the window. A gust of wind blows the curtains. SALOMON returns his attention to the book, opening it, and paging through it. He finds a photo between the pages, which he takes out and studies. A tear trails down his cheek. Slowly, almost ceremonial, he closes the book and, holding it like his most treasured possession, he carries it with* him out of the hotel room. As he walks, his limp comes across worse than before.)

(IDA gets up, uncertain of herself, her movements are slow and heavy. She places a hand over her stomach as if resenting the life that has been taken from her womb. She goes to the window with an almost automatic pace. Once there, an enraged IDA takes off the bathrobe and throws it on the bed. Before climbing up onto the windowsill, she reaches back to run her fingers over her shoulder, as if to ensure that her burn marks are still there. Once on the windowsill, IDA waits a moment. The air blows her hair and almost causes her to lose her balance. Suddenly, she realizes that she does not want to hold on any longer. IDA allows herself to fall.)

(The stage now appears as it did at the beginning. A gust of wind again blows the curtains. Suddenly, outside a woman screams from the street level ten floors below. A cloud softens the invading sunlight. Silence. The door opens. SALOMON enters with a suitcase, the same one he carried in the beginning. Behind him enters HANNA again. She remains a suspicious woman watching her every step as if she feared the floor would fall out from under her feet.)

SALOMON (*Indignant*): The best hotel in town. Isn't that what they said? The best hotel in town and they make you carry your own luggage to your room. (*To HANNA.*) Come in, come in. Don't stay out there. They'll think that . . . Just, come in. (*HANNA enters and closes the door, but does not sit. SALOMON notices the disheveled sheets with a white bathrobe on top of them. He leaves his suitcase on the floor and sets a stack of papers on the table.*) And on top of that. Who the hell is running this place? (*To HANNA.*) Did you hear what they said about this room? You were right there with me. The best suite of the best hotel in town. Now I've seen it all.

HANNA: Things are different here than in your country, Mr. Salomon.

SALOMON: Unfortunately, things here are different than in any other country in the world. (*SALOMON looks about the room with disgust. He turns toward the window suddenly as if something were calling his attention. For a moment, he is taken with fear.*)

HANNA: Are you all right, Mr. Salomon?

(*Curtain.*)

ABOUT THE TRANSLATOR

DJ Sanders has also translated Guillem Clua's *Taste of Ashes* (from the original Spanish *El sabor de las cenizas*) and Àngel Guimerà's 1896 classic *The Lowlands* (from the original Catalan *Terra Baixa*). Sanders is the author of more than twenty stage plays, including *The Damascus Trilogy* (an adaptation of Strindberg's *To Damascus, I-III*) and *White Horses* (a prequel to Ibsen's *Rosmersholm*). Sanders previously taught advanced English for non-native speakers at the University of Illinois, the University of Barcelona, and Washington University in St. Louis. He is currently pursuing further graduate studies at Washington University in St. Louis focusing on the translation of drama. He is a member of the Dramatists Guild. More information on Sanders' plays and translations is available at www.djsanders.com.

TRANSLATOR'S ACKNOWLEDGMENTS

I would like to thank Marion Peter Holt for encouraging me to take on this, my first translation project, and for his continued support that has allowed this translation to be published. Special thanks to Guillem Clua for granting me permission to translate his play, providing timely feedback, and becoming a valued friend in the process. Many thanks to Jason Cannon, HotCity Theatre, and everyone involved in both the initial reading and the U.S. premiere production of *Skin in Flames*. And I especially want to thank my partner, Tom Hake, for all of his love and support as I have taken on translation.

CRITICAL REACTION TO THE PLAY

"The work does diverge slightly from the canon of 'war dramas' because there is not one single explicit reference to the country in which this story takes place. Of importance is not the place of the military conflict, but its very existence, and also because during the time of action decades have already passed since the bombs were falling. But its inspiration is easily recognized through the plot in which the protagonists discuss a photograph, which clearly alludes to the famous image captured by Vietnamese photographer, Nick Ut, during an explosion of napalm, with a little girl running naked with her skin burned."

Belén Ginart
El País, 2005

"[*Skin in Flames*] has a balanced structure confined to two interrelated couples representing dominance and vulnerability, both scenes synchronized to play in two rooms of a hotel, with a revolving exposition that draws focus to one space or the other. The dialogue is dry and heartless yet dramatically sound."

Maria-José Rague-Arias
El Mundo, 2005

"Anyone attending *Skin in Flames* is advised to wear asbestos clothes. This intense Spanish drama by Guillem Clua…ignites a theatrical wildfire of suspense and surprise that sears the imagination."

Dennis Brown
Riverfront Times, 2006

"Without specifying concrete nations or wars, Clua, who plays with the coordination of time and space, has used this situation in an enriching theatrical game, placing four characters in one hotel room, allowing two couples to converse amongst themselves without any acknowledgement of the presence of the other couple because—and the audience with grasp this immediately—presumably these conversations are taking place at distinct times."

Elena Hevia
El Periódico, 2005

"This is a rare opportunity to see a thoughtful and refreshingly different perspective on the relationship between the First World and the Third World in the context of war. Although there are revelations in this play that will undoubtedly make even some of the most well-intentioned liberal theatergoers feel uncomfortable, any such discomfort can only be a sign of a functioning conscience, and is an essentially healthy, if not entirely pleasant, response to the play's content."

Daniel Higgins
KDHX Theatre Review, 2006

"Filled with gut-wrenching twists, *Skin in Flames* takes the audience on an emotional and intellectual journey challenging them to consider and question the fine line dividing those in power and those in need of assistance. With the expertly crafted structure and story elements found in every country's newspaper headlines, *Skin in Flames* melds the best of content and form into a hauntingly unforgettable theatrical experience."

Theatre Alliance of Greater Philadelphia, 2007

ESTRENO: CONTEMPORARY SPANISH PLAYS SERIES

No. 1 Jaime Salom: ***Bonfire at Dawn*** *(Una hoguera al amanecer)*
Translated by Phyllis Zatlin. Rev. ed. 2006.
ISBN: 1-888463-23-6 / 978-1-888463-23-1

No. 2 José López Rubio: ***In August We Play the Pyrenees*** *(Celos del aire)*
Translated by Marion Peter Holt. 1992.
ISBN: 0-9631212-1-9

No. 3 Ramón del Valle-Inclán: ***Savage Acts: Four Plays*** *(Ligazón, La rosa de papel, La cabeza del Bautista, Sacrilegio)*
Translated by Robert Lima. 1993.
ISBN: 0-9631212-2-7

No. 4 Antonio Gala: ***The Bells of Orleans*** *(Los buenos días perdidos)*
Translated by Edward Borsoi. 1993.
ISBN: 0-9631212-3-5

No. 5 Antonio Buero-Vallejo: ***The Music Window*** *(Música cercana)*
Translated by Marion Peter Holt. 1994.
ISBN: 0-9631212-4-3

No. 6 Paloma Pedrero: ***Parting Gestures*** with ***A Night in the Subway*** *(El color de agosto, La noche dividida, Resguardo personal, Solos esta noche)*
Translated by Phyllis Zatlin. Revised ed. 1999.
ISBN: 1-888463-06-6

No. 7 Ana Diosdado: ***Yours for the Asking*** *(Usted también podrá disfrutar de ella)*
Translated by Patricia W. O'Connor. 1995.
ISBN: 0-9631212-6-X

No. 8 Manuel Martínez Mediero: ***A Love Too Beautiful*** *(Juana del amor hermoso)*
Translated by Hazel Cazorla. 1995.
ISBN: 0-9631212-7-8

No. 9 Alfonso Vallejo: ***Train to Kiu*** *(El cero transparente)*
Translated by H. Rick Hite. 1996. ISBN: 0-9631212-8-6

No. 10 Alfonso Sastre: ***The Abandoned Doll. Young Billy Tell***. (*Historia de una muñeca abandonada. El único hijo de William Tell*).
Translated by Carys Evans-Corrales. 1996.
ISBN: 1-888463-00-7

No. 11 Lauro Olmo and Pilar Encisco: ***The Lion Calls a Meeting. The Lion Foiled. The Lion in Love***. (*Asamblea general. Los leones*)
Translated by Carys Evans-Corrales. 1997.
ISBN: 1-888463-01-5

No. 12 José Luis Alonso de Santos: ***Hostages in the Barrio***. (*La estanquera de Vallecas*).
Translated by Phyllis Zatlin. 1997.
ISBN: 1-888463-02-3

No. 13 Fermín Cabal: ***Passage***. (*Travesía*)
Translated by H. Rick Hite. 1998.
ISBN: 1-888463-03-1

No. 14 Antonio Buero-Vallejo: ***The Sleep of Reason*** (*El sueño de la razón*)
Translated by Marion Peter Holt. 1998.
ISBN: 1-888463-04-X

No. 15 Fernando Arrabal: ***The Body-Builder's Book of Love*** (*Breviario de amor de un halterófilo*)
Translated by Lorenzo Mans. 1999.
ISBN: 1-888463-05-8

No. 16 Luis Araújo: ***Vanzetti***
Translated by Mary-Alice Lessing. 1999.
ISBN: 1-888463-08-2

No. 17 Josep M. Benet i Jornet: ***Legacy*** (*Testament*)
Translated by Janet DeCesaris. 2000.
ISBN: 1-888463-09-0

No. 18 Sebastián Junyent: ***Packing up the Past*** (*Hay que deshacer la casa*)
Translated by Ana Mengual. 2000.
ISBN: 1-888463-10-4

No. 19 Paloma Pedrero: ***First Star & The Railing*** *(Una estrella & El pasamanos)*
Translated by H. Rick Hite. 2001.
ISBN: 1-888463-11-2

No. 20 José María Rodríguez Méndez: ***Autumn Flower*** *(Flor de Otoño)*
Translated by Marion Peter Holt. 2001.
ISBN: 1-888463-12-0

No. 21 Juan Mayorga: ***Love Letters to Stalin*** *(Cartas de amor a Stalin)*
Translated by María E. Padilla. 2002.
ISBN: 1-888463-13-9

No. 22 Eduardo Galán & Javier Garcimartín: ***Inn Discretions*** *(La posada del Arenal)*
Translated by Leonardo Mazzara. 2002.
ISBN: 1-888463-14-7

No. 23 Beth Escudé i Gallès: ***Killing Time & Keeping in Touch*** *(El color del gos quan fuig & La lladre i la Sra Guix)*
Translated by Bethany M. Korp & Janet DeCesaris. 2003.
ISBN: 1-888463-15-5

No. 24 José Sanchis Sinisterra: ***The Siege of Leningrad*** *(El cerco de Leningrado)*
Translated by Mary-Alice Lessing. 2003.
ISBN: 1-888463-16-3

No. 25 Sergi Belbel: ***Blood*** *(La sang)*
Translated by Marion Peter Holt. 2004.
ISBN: 1-888463-17-1

No. 26 Cristina Fernández Cubas: ***Blood Sisters*** *(Hermanas de sangre)*
Translated by Karen Denise Dinicola. 2004.
ISBN: 1-888463-18-X

No. 27 Ignacio del Moral: ***Dark Man's Gaze and Other Plays*** (*La mirada del hombre oscuro. Papis. Osesnos*)
Translated by Jartu Gallashaw Toles. 2005.
ISBN: 1-888463-19-8

No. 28 Concha Romero: ***A Saintly Scent of Amber*** (*Un olor a ámbar*)
Translated by Karen Leahy. 2005.
ISBN: 1-888463-20-1 / 978-1-888463-20-0

No. 29 Itziar Pascual: ***Gone Astray: Castaways, Holiday Out, Meowless*** (*Varadas, Holliday Aut, Miauless*)
Translated by Phyllis Zatlin. 2006.
ISBN: 1-888463-24-4 / 978-1-888463-24-8

No. 30 Ana Diosdado, Paloma Pedrero & Yolanda Dorado: **Staging Terror: Madrid 3/11. Harira, Ana 3/11, Oxygen** (*Harira, Ana el once de marzo, Oxígeno*)
Translated by Karen Leahy and Phyllis Zatlin. 2007
ISBN: 978-1-888463-25-5

No. 31 Guillem Clua: **Skin in Flames** (*La pell en flames*)
Translated by DJ Sanders, 2008.
ISBN: 978-1-888463-27-9

ORDER AND CONTACT INFORMATION

ESTRENO Plays
c/o Iride Lamartina-Lens
   Susan Berardini
Modern Languages Dept., PNY
Pace University
41 Park Row
New York, NY 10038 USA

Phone: 1-212-346-1433 or 1432
E-mail: ilamartinalens@pace.edu
          sberardini@pace.edu
Fax: 1-212-346-1435

VISIT OUR WEBSITE:

www.rci.rutgers.edu/~estrplay/webpage.html

ESTRENO Plays was founded in 1992 by Martha T. Halsey at Penn State University. In 1998-99 the series moved to Rutgers, The State University of New Jersey, where it was edited by Phyllis Zatlin. Starting in 2005-2006, it has been co-edited by Iride Lamartina-Lens and Susan Berardini, professors at Pace University in Manhattan.

ESTRENO Plays is printed at Ag Press in Manhattan, Kansas.